Making the
Big Leap

7 Steps to living a
Brave, Inspired
and Great Life

SUZY GREAVES

To Charlie

This edition first published in 2010 by New Holland Publishers (UK) Ltd
London • Cape Town • Sydney • Auckland
www.newhollandpublishers.com

Garfield House, 86–88 Edgware Road, London W2 2EA, United Kingdom
80 McKenzie Street, Cape Town 8001, South Africa
Unit 1, 66 Gibbes Street, Chatswood, NSW 2067, Australia
218 Lake Road, Northcote, Auckland, New Zealand

10 9 8 7 6 5 4 3 2 1

A catalogue record for this book is available from the British Library

ISBN 978 1 84773 680 2

Publisher: Jo Hemmings, Aruna Vasudevan
Editors: Deborah Taylor, Charlotte Judet, Kate Parker
Cover design: Paul Wright
Design: Phil Kay
Production: Melanie Dowland

Reproduction by Modern Age
Printed and bound in India by Replika Press Pvt Ltd

Read this book if:

- You get on the treadmill every morning and think, 'There has to be another way.'

- You've just had your own personal wake-up call, and you're committed to finding a new way to live your life.

- You find yourself thinking regularly, 'I just can't do this anymore.'

- You don't want to struggle any more; you want to find a life that delights you.

- You are prepared to think differently, not just do something different.

- You are prepared to be the creator of your life, not the victim of it.

- You want a life that you adore.

Contents

The Big Beginning: 'I can't do this anymore'

Thirteen years ago, I woke up...

I woke up dribbling on a stranger's shoulder 30 miles from home at the end of the train line, having slept through my stop, and thought, 'I can't do this anymore.' I was a journalist and worked 16 hours a day, 6 days a week: grind, grind, non-stop. I was tired. All the time. My whole day was spent fighting a bone-crushing fatigue that seemed to eat me up from the inside out until all I could do was cushion myself on the sofa every night lest the slightest knock shatter me into tiny, brittle pieces.

Waking up with two other snoring strangers at the end of a train line in the wilds of Essex, I felt like I'd found myself in an elephant's graveyard. Except it was where commuters went to die.

How had life turned into this great war? And, more to the point, why was I losing? From the outside, it didn't look like I was. Life looked great. I was married to a man I loved, I had the job of my dreams writing for glossy magazines, and an apartment with my husband in a trendy part of London. I had everything I thought I wanted, so why was life this hard? Why was I so damn tired all the time? Why did I feel this gnawing discontent that had me crawling into a bottle of wine every night to make me feel better? Coffee to get me going, then cigarettes to keep me going, and a bottle of wine in the evening to make me stop.

I woke up on the train that night and knew that if I accepted this as just how life is, I'd be on that track for the rest of my life, constantly fighting to stay out of the commuter's graveyard. And I didn't want to struggle any more. That evening, I woke up and thought, 'NO.' I wanted to shake my fellow commuters awake and scream, 'It doesn't have to be this way. It doesn't, it doesn't, it doesn't!' But I wasn't really screaming at them, I was screaming at myself. It was this silent scream that woke me up.

I realize now that a 'big' life was calling me. I don't mean 'big' as in livin' it large, with a bigger house, a faster car and a more important job title. I mean BIG as in living in our most expanded place, where everything is possible, where we are guided by something bigger than fear, comparison and ambition.

When I woke up 13 years ago, I was living 'small' – squashed in a compartment, trapped in a life someone else thought I should live. And I didn't want that any more. On some level, I knew I wanted to leap, to expand, to grow, to come from a brave, inspired place and live a great life rather than one lived in exhaustion, fear and struggle. But it felt like that was the only way I knew how to live.

I needed help, so I hired a coach: a Life Coach. I know it sounds too 'Oprah' for words, and being a 'tell-it-like-it-is' Northerner, I had similar prejudices. But who better to help me on my quest for a new life? Now, of course, I'm a convert. In fact, I was so impressed that I bought the company, as it were. I trained to become a coach myself and set up my own coaching company.

Thirteen years ago, I told my coach, 'I can't do this anymore.'

She didn't ask what 'this' was, but asked what I wanted instead.

'I want a life I adore,' I said. 'A life with plenty of time, money, space, lots of lovely friends, a job you'd pay to do. I want to bubble over again. I want to sing in the shower. I want my bounce back.'

What I wanted was a life full of love, space and freedom, to be nuzzled non-stop by my husband, to spend holidays on a palm-lined beach in the Caribbean, never to have to screen telephone calls to avoid speaking to so-called friends who vampire every ounce of energy left after a gruelling day. No more gruelling days – just work that would make every day feel like a holiday. I was sick of being in debt and never, ever catching up. I didn't want to feel tired, fed up and as if I was dragging myself around life. I wanted to feel content, peaceful and 'in' my life rather than on the outside desperately looking through a window.

I got excited for a second before reality elbowed me firmly in the ribs. Content? Peaceful? I couldn't afford a holiday to Cardiff, never mind the Caribbean. My husband was more into guzzling beer than nuzzling me. Every day like a holiday? Who was I kidding? Then came the question that changed my life. 'What would you have to believe about yourself for this dream to come true?'

I blustered, I sneered, I sneered a bit more, but in the end I wept. I realized that for me to live a BIG life, a life of courage and inspiration, the thing that was going to have to change was me. I didn't believe in me. I didn't believe I was good enough, clever enough, beautiful enough, witty enough, anything enough to manifest even a tiny piece of my dream life.

That question was my gateway into the place where I got my bounce back. It made me realize that if I wanted to transform my external world, I'd have to change my internal one. Through my own journey, and from coaching hundreds of my own clients, I have discovered that if you don't believe you're good enough and you listen to the voice of fear that beats you up regularly, you can't say 'No.' You put up with stuff you don't want to put up with. You work all day and night to prove that you are worthy of a place in the world.

This book is for those who want to think big. It is for those who are sick of 'living it little', feeling boxed in, like somehow you are living the wrong life. This book is about finding another way. It's about the courage to live a life that inspires, fulfils and delights you.

Making the Big Leap is about shaking up your whole life and finding a new way of working, living and being. Maybe you don't want to commute any more and prefer to work from home. Perhaps you want to live in another country. Maybe you want to fall in love at seventy, or write a novel in your sixties, or start a freelance career when you hit fifty that pays for who you are, not just for what you do. Or maybe you want to give it all up and live a radically different life.

My clients have wanted many things: to leave the corporate world behind to write, to leave their conventional lives behind to explore a different way of living, to live by the beach with sand between their toes, or to create a global brand based on their personal passion for handbags. But most of all, each sought to be happy, fulfilled and passionate about their work, their life and the people they share their life with.

I believe Big Leapers are pioneers of a new groundswell of voices shouting, 'No, enough! We don't have to live this way, we don't have to sell our souls, sell our dreams, commute three hours a day, never see our kids and loved ones and slowly fritter away our lives.' Big Leapers are holding up a light, laughing and leading the way, shouting, 'Don't compromise, there is another way. Let's do it our way, let's create it the way we want, let's live on our terms.'

Making the Big Leap is a handbook for the Big Leap generation. It's a map to help you on your journey. We have left the 20th century behind, and with it, the rules that told us how to sit, behave and live our lives. We now have the freedom to choose a life and create it any way we want. But that freedom comes with a price. As we are no longer told what we 'should' be doing, we are left with uncertainty, which makes us question ourselves constantly about our choices – 'Am I doing this right? Is my way wrong? Am I simply fooling myself?'

This book will hopefully keep you sane and will hold your hand along the way. What it offers is not so much a how-to process, but rather a guide, shining the light of awareness on fears and blocks so you will be better equipped to steer a path around them.

The seven-step Big Leap journey

I have created a map to give you some useful signposts to follow on your Big Leap journey. In my own journey to living my 'Big' life, I have been writing fiction, and in the process, reading many how-to books on creating story structure. My story-writing bible has been *Save the Cat! The Last Book on Screenwriting You'll Ever Need*, which was written by my good friend and mentor, the Hollywood guru Blake Snyder, who has now sadly passed away. His famous 15-beat (-element) story structure is not only a guide to screenwriting, but also for life. He said:

All stories are about transformation. All stories are the caterpillar turning into a butterfly in some sense. All stories require a death and rebirth to make that painful and glorious process happen. And it occurs in movies ... and in life. We transform every day, re-awaken to new concepts about the world around us, overcome conflict,

and triumph over death ... only to start again each
morning. It's why stories that follow this pattern
resonate. Because each day is a transformation
machine and so are our lives.

I have adapted Blake's story structure into a seven-step
Big Leap journey.

You are the hero of your own story, with all the ticks,
tricks, heartbreaks and bad habits that we usually
encounter when introduced to the main character in a
novel or a film. In the first part of a story, the hero (that's
you!) usually confronts a catalyst that rocks their old
world, shaking them out of the status quo thinking of
'That's just how things are.'

The hero is then invited to make the leap after someone
or something (be it a baddie boss, a heartbreak, an illness,
a promotion) challenges them to take action and step into
a whole new world. (Think Dorothy desperately trying to
save her dog Toto from her horrible neighbour and
getting blown away by the cyclone into the Land of Oz.)

The first part of the journey into this new world can be
fun, as the hero gets to know the new terrain and makes
friends with their proverbial Scarecrow, Cowardly Lion
and Tin Man. But just when they begin to feel they're
'winning', they start to hit more difficult obstacles, be
they internal fears or external manifestations – like the
Wicked Witch of the West throwing fireballs at their best
friend made of straw.

The hero battles these fears and obstacles and is challenged
to a point where they think they cannot go on. Blake calls
this the 'rock-bottom' moment. Usually the hero is worse
off than they were at the beginning of the story – broke,
heartbroken, their worst fears confirmed. The Wicked

Witch has captured the hero in her castle and is threatening to throw their pet dog off the cliff. This is usually the moment of transformation where they 'find a way', transforming their fears and bouncing back to the finale of the story (usually with a little help from their friends – when the Cowardly Lion decides not to be so cowardly and the hero melts the Wicked Witch with a bucket of water). Oh yes, it all happens in that grand finale!

I'm a big fan of *The Wizard of Oz* because I believe it's the ultimate transformation story. The Big Leap journey follows Dorothy's adventure almost to the letter. Dorothy yearns for a life over the rainbow, as she lives her colourless life in Kansas with her Auntie Em and Uncle Henry. A cyclone then magically carries her off to the Land of Oz, where she goes in search of the Wizard of Oz with her friends, the Scarecrow, the Tin Man and the Cowardly Lion, who symbolize Dorothy's brain, heart and courage, which she must call upon to find her way back 'home'.

At the beginning of her journey, she looks to the magical Wizard of Oz to give her the answers, but with the help of Glinda, the Good Witch of the North, Dorothy realizes she has everything she needs to make the leap herself. I believe we all have an inner Glinda in our lives, which I call the Inner Coach – but more on him/her later!

Of course, the story wouldn't be complete without a baddie, the Wicked Witch of the West, who vows, 'I'll get you, my pretty, and your little dog, too!' She does everything she can to sabotage Dorothy and her friends on their journey. I believe we all meet our 'inner' Wicked Witch on our Big Leap journey. I call him/her your Inner Pessimist. We'll be meeting him very soon.

The story of the Wizard of Oz outlines the journey we all go on when we make the Big Leap. We have to travel to strange lands, face all sorts of obstacles and be very brave in order to discover that we have everything we need within us to get to where we want to go.

The Big Leap to a more fulfilled, happier, 'big' life is not always easy, but it's always an adventure. Ultimately it's about transformation. Sometimes you don't actually get what you think you want at the end of your journey, but what you learn about yourself along the way can change your life forever – in a good way.

I wish I could tell you that *Making the Big Leap* is a seven-step quick-fix programme – after all, it might sell faster! But if I did, I'd be lying. It takes time to shift your internal landscape so your external scenery can start to look different. I know we're all searching for the magic pill that will transform life overnight, but this book is not going to give you any false promises. It's not going to dress it up for you and tell you that it's quick and easy, because sometimes it's not, and it's okay that it's not. Making the Big Leap requires courage, determination and the ability to laugh at yourself – a lot. The exercises in this book can be life changing but the journey is not a fluffy then-I-woke-up-and-my-life-was-different kind of trip. If only …

On this journey, you'll be confronting yourself and coming up against questions that you've probably been avoiding for years. To make the Big Leap, you'll probably have to step way out of your comfort zone and be prepared to feel out of your depth, grumpy and downright terrified at times. But don't panic! Each Big Step is split up into many baby steps. I'm a big believer in baby steps. When you're gripped by fear, you can always take a baby step, and that's when the magic happens. That's how you start building your courage so you become strong enough to make the Big Leap. And watch how life comes out to greet you. Not once, but every time.

Seven steps on the Big Leap journey

Step 1

Moan about the Big Blah
'Somewhere over the rainbow'
You moan and groan about what you don't want in your life any more and yearn for something different.

Step 2

Hear the Big Wake-up Call
'It's a twister, it's a twister!'
Someone or something demands that you change. This is your catalyst moment – be it a baddie boss, a job loss, or the Wicked Witch of the West, often we only choose (or are forced) to take action when a situation becomes unbearable.

Step 3

Enter the Big New World
'We're not in Kansas any more.'
You begin to discover a new world and figure out what your real purpose is: what you really want versus what everyone else wants for you (with a little help from Glinda, your Good Witch of the North, or your Inner Coach, as I call her).

Step 4

Find the Big Belief
'We're off to see the Wizard, the Wonderful Wizard of Oz.'
You know what you want and you're going for it, at first believing that an external 'something' can give you what

you want – be it money, fame, love. You gradually discover that you have everything you need inside of yourself to make the Big Leap and live a 'big' life. You begin to explore your belief systems to find out what's holding you back.

Step 5

Face the Big Baddie

'They sure knocked the stuffing out of you, didn't they?'
In *The Wizard of Oz*, flying monkeys come and carry Dorothy away, trying to destroy her friendships and her hope. On the Big Leap journey, you will discover your very own flying monkeys – your little scams – the behaviours and actions that keep you stuck.

Step 6

Sink into the Big Low

'I'm frightened, Auntie Em! I'm frightened!'
You hit rock bottom, feel the fear, and face failure as you are locked up in a metaphorical castle in your head. You need to rescue yourself quickly.

Step 7

Make the Big Leap

'Tap your heels together.'
Finally, you realize that you have everything you need to take the next step. To get to where you really want to be, all you have to do is take action.

Keeping a Big Leap journal

To get the most out of your journey, I suggest that you create a Big Leap journal. Get a special notebook in which you can write down your answers to the many questions and exercises in this book. You'll find it will be be helpful to have all your 'answers' in the same place rather than on the backs of envelopes or scraps of paper scattered around the house. It's also great to look back on, to see how far you've come and also to see patterns that emerge. I still find it highly encouraging to look back at my own Big Leap journal – the journey of despair from waking up on a train in the wilds of the countryside to retraining for a career that inspires me every day and fills me with so much energy that it feels like my hair is standing on end.

Let's begin … *'Somewhere over the rainbow'*

Just before you start making your seven-step journey, I need you to make a commitment – a commitment to suspending belief of what you know of the world so far, a commitment to preparing yourself to enter a world where anything is possible. 'Yeah, yeah, whatever,' you might say. But what if by thinking different thoughts, we could also create a new world of transformation and truth?

At this point in the Big Leap process, you're probably a bit dubious, so all I'm asking you to do right now is to commit to being open to finding this 'other' world, this other way of being. When I woke up on that train all those years ago, I decided that I couldn't live life in a way that exhausted me and seemed to drain my very soul. I knew then that I was going to find another way. I was going to think differently. I was going to 'do' differently, but I didn't have a clue what that meant. At that point, I simply had to commit to the idea that I would find out.

Unfortunately, sometimes it has to get really bad before we decide we've had enough of doing things the old way. Sometimes it takes a life-threatening illness, the death of a loved one or a misery that seems to seep into our very soul for us to make the decision to live another way. Maybe life is about as bad as it can possibly get and you've been living in fear of the Wicked Witch for too long. Or maybe you've picked up this book because things are simply jogging along, day after day. Or perhaps you've got the shiny red car, the house in the country and the career that allows you to go on three holidays a year, but you feel all you've got is the lifestyle, but not the life. Or maybe you just know this can't be all there is.

Whether it's just a vague discontent or the horror of discovering you've got breast cancer – whether it's the whisper or the roar you've heard – I'm assuming you're in the process of searching for some answers or you wouldn't have bought this book. That's a big step in itself. So now, before you start, make a commitment to be open to thinking differently, and maybe a little bit magically. Be willing to learn a different way of doing things, to enter another world where magic can happen, where you leave 'Kansas' behind and recreate everything you've believed about life so far in the way you want.

Before you close the book, thinking that I'm trying to get you to join a cult, wear a pointed hat and run naked round the garden, let me spell it out in the ten points that follow:

10 ways to know you're willing to live and think magically

1. You don't know 'how' life is going to change, you just know it will.
2. You feel very, very excited.

3. You feel very, very scared.
4. You are willing to reinvent the way you see the world.
5. You are willing to reinvent the way you see yourself.
6. You are willing to see it when you believe it.
7. You know that life is just about to get a whole lot different.
8. Deep down you know you have a lot of hidden potential.
9. Deep down you know you are very powerful.
10. Deep down you believe in magic.

When I woke up on that train all those years ago, I would never have thought a life like this was possible. But I knew with every fibre of my being that there was another way. Now I know for sure that none of us needs to live a life that bores us, exhausts us, or drains every ounce of energy from our soul. We can create the lives we want. We just need to rethink them and find the courage to get out of our comfort zones.

The way to start this process is to answer some tough questions, decide to stop being a victim, and to stop blaming everyone and everything else for what our life is and to then start making some different choices. Choices that align us with a different kind of energy – the energy of hope, of hilarity, of happiness. Choices that give us an energy that blows our hair back and makes us remember why we're alive and what our purpose is.

The hardest step is always the first – it means taking responsibility for your life and knowing that only you can change it. It is a Big Leap, and it is momentous and life-altering. But it is also a magical journey. So, now, if you are ready to take your first step to make the Big Leap, if you're ready to commit, if you're ready to rewrite your story, I suggest you have your wand at the ready. Turn the page to meet your support team and then begin.

The Big Leap cheerleaders

Because the Big Leap journey can be lonely at times, I've invited some guests along. Think about them as your very own Scarecrow, Tin Man and Cowardly Lion to keep you company along the way. I have asked 11 of my clients who have made or are in the process of making the Big Leap to give their best advice, practical tips and words of wisdom. Meet your Big Leap support team.

Nicky Hambleton-Jones, 37, came to coaching in January 2001. A management consultant, she was made redundant in the first week of our coaching together. It was the third time this had happened to Nicky. Never wanting to find herself in this position again, she dreamed about creating her own business in something she was passionate about. Nicky chose fashion, and I coached her in starting her own fashion-styling business, website and brand. In 2003, she was signed by Channel 4 in the UK to present her own TV show on transforming others to look 10 years younger. She is currently working on creating a global anti-ageing business.

Marc Lockley, 42, worked 60 hours a week earning a six-figure salary as Head of Agency Sales at the *Daily Mail*. He came to coaching in September 2005. He sought more work–life balance and decided to leave his job to create a 'portfolio' career. He now runs his own coaching company, Lockley Associates, is 'The Negotiator' columnist for the UK online newspaper the *Guardian*, and has written and published the book *How to Pay Less for More*.

Lynne McNicoll, 52, had not worked for eight years when she first hired me as her coach in September 2002. She sought coaching primarily because she wanted to find new motivation to lose weight. Lynne was a housewife living in Edinburgh when we started working together. Six months later, she had made the Big Leap and created her own business working from home as a 'virtual assistant', a PA who works for many clients, handling their needs through email and the Internet. Through her work, Lynne became interested in fundraising for the Teenage Cancer Trust and spent her fiftieth year raising £50,000 for charity. Her current challenge is to raise £500,000 by the end of 2009.

Rachel Dobson, 35, came to coaching in May 2003. A senior features writer for a national Sunday tabloid, Rachel decided she wanted to leave the nine-to-five lifestyle behind and create a freelance business. She handed in her notice in August 2003 and is currently a freelance features journalist, as well as a mum. She is also setting up her own business as a property developer with an international property portfolio.

Tracy L'Epine, 42, was a stuntwoman who decided to change career because she wanted to have a baby. At 40 she had become pregnant, but miscarried. This inspired her to look into alternative approaches to getting and staying pregnant. Using these approaches, Tracy became pregnant and is now mother to her beautiful daughter Rosie Moon. Tracy then started her company MindBodyBaby, a website with resources and products for women who want to get pregnant naturally and to help people recover from miscarriage.

Anne Thorn, 53, is an IT project manager in London. She brought up her son on her own, and when he left home to go to university, Anne was lonely and frustrated, feeling she lacked a social life. Anne came to coaching in September 2007. She decided to set up the website www.e4friends.co.uk to create a social club for people in her area and now has a very vibrant social life.

Andrew Stone, 38, was a journalist on a trade magazine in London. In September 2000, he made the Big Leap, resigning from his job and setting off for Hong Kong to find writing work there. Andrew is now writing for Lonely Planet, travelling to destinations including Ireland, South Africa and Australia.

Keris Stainton, 38, had been working in corporate recovery and personal insolvency (which, according to her, is just as soul destroying as it sounds!) and dreaming of writing a novel. Within weeks of coming for coaching, she realized that she wanted to revive her teenage ambition to become a journalist. She quickly received two commissions with a national glossy magazine and then gave up work to write full time. She has since had articles published in a number of magazines. Keris has also finished a young adult novel *Della Says: OMG! WTF?* and signed a two-book deal with a major publisher.

Ann Norton, 57, was living in Melbourne and desperately wanted to move to London. She hired a coach in 2007, and within six months had bought a plane ticket, resigned from her job at her university in Melbourne and packed up her things, moving in 2008. She found a job within four months and now lives in her favourite area in London.

Jules Ritter, 45, was a full-time mother and wife living in Switzerland and struggling with 'empty-nest syndrome' when she came to coaching in 2008. She wanted to build on her talent for writing and become a successful freelance journalist and writer. She has since gone on to be published in magazines, newspapers and various websites, and has her own blog, One writer's life.

Irene Brankin, 65, psychologist and coach, came to me for coaching in May 2009. Her goal is to relaunch her business running self-development courses and write a book on 'the call of the wise woman' – how older women can stop being invisible, rekindle passion for life and start new adventures. Irene is a survivor of bowel cancer.

The Big Blah
*'Somewhere over
the rainbow'*

*'It's never too late to be what
you might have been'*
– GEORGE ELIOT,
ENGLISH NOVELIST (1819–80)

> **Big Leap Step 1:   THE BABY STEPS**
>
> 1. The boiled-frog syndrome
> 2. Victim City
> 3. Meet your Inner Pessimist

'There has to be more to life than this ...' is the first step of your journey towards making the Big Leap. This is the part where you're stuck in Kansas and yearning for another life 'over the rainbow'. I will be asking you to really look your life in the eye and get very real about what is not working for you. It's a challenging process, and it can feel a tad depressing. You may end up wondering why you're doing it, but you'll know exactly why once it's done, and you'll certainly be ready to make some changes. Make sure you don't wallow in this step too long though. The purpose is to move you out of pain and into action, to move on quickly so you can discover how to be who you want to be and do what you want to do.

What you're probably thinking at Big Leap Step 1

- There has to be more to life than this.
- What am I doing with my life?
- How on earth did I get here?
- I want more!
- I want it all.
- I want to live 'over the rainbow'.

What you're probably doing at Big Leap Step 1

- You go to the bar or pub after work a lot or find yourself drinking at home every night.
- You feel envious of other people's lives and bitch about them to your friends.
- You find yourself obsessively watching TV shows about how to change your life/garden/house.
- You buy 10 lottery tickets every week.
- You watch more than 10 hours of TV a week.
- You're always busy, but never feel as if you're achieving a great deal.
- You feel a vague sense of discontent, even in your happiest moments.
- You're doing everything, but going nowhere.
- You're doing nothing and live in a paralyzed state of inaction and apathy.

The first step in the Big Leap seven-step programme is to come out of denial, come out of the fog and get very clear about what you don't want. At this point, you don't have to do anything about it – just tell the truth.

Maybe you have lived in denial for years, numbing yourself with alcohol or cigarettes or by watching so much TV that you know the storyline of every soap there is – even the really bad ones! 'How are things?' people ask you. 'You know, okay,' you say. You stagger from one weekend to the next, vaguely discontent, but not quite being able to put your finger on why. Or maybe you can … Maybe you blame your misery on your crap boss, or your partner who seems to have lost their sparkle, or those extra pounds of weight that you simply can't shift because deep down, you know that if you really admitted what was wrong, you would have to do something about it. So don't underestimate how much courage it takes to come out of denial and admit your life stinks.

Like Kate, for instance, who had to admit that she hated her career after spending years in training. She was 32 and had spent seven years studying to be a doctor, but found herself in the bar most nights. 'I just drank and drank. I was desperately unhappy, but couldn't admit why. I hated my job, but I couldn't admit it to anyone, least of all myself, because that meant I'd have to do something about it and that scared me to death.' I asked Kate not to think past this first step. All she had to do was admit the truth about her life as it was now.

'I've just spent my twenties training for a career that gives me prestige and respect in the outside world, but I hate every minute, every second of it. I've never wanted to be a doctor. I even hated biology when I was at school. I don't want to be a doctor any more.' There. It was out – the bare, bald truth of it. Scary stuff; but also liberating for her to say it out loud for the first time.

When we constantly hide the truth about a situation and live in denial – whether it be about our relationships ('I don't love you any more.') or our career ('I can't do this anymore.') or our money situation ('I'm £30,000 in debt.'), it's like a hole at the bottom of our lives that drains every ounce of our energy, enthusiasm and passion. No matter whether we eat the right foods or sleep the right amount of hours or drink our daily eight glasses of water, if we live in denial of what's really not working in our lives, we become so drained of energy that we find ourselves using stimulants or creating dramas or crises to try and jump-start us out of bed every morning.

Nicky Hambleton-Jones, Big Leaping from management consultant to celebrity fashion stylist

When I first came to coaching I was exhausted, trying to fit myself into a lifestyle and job that I hated. I was a management consultant. From the outside, it probably looked like I had a glamorous life but I hated it. I felt stupid and worthless and simply didn't fit into the value systems of the company I worked for. I'd find myself working harder and harder, only to feel more insecure. All I'd do was work all the time. I didn't have time to see my friends or even think about finding a boyfriend.

I hired Suzy, my coach, to try and help me work out where I was going wrong. In my first week of coaching, I was made redundant. It was the third time this had happened to me. I bawled my eyes out. I felt so lost and unhappy. I thought, 'That's it, I've failed, I'm useless.' I had this awful period of a month where I was forced out of denial by the redundancy. I had to admit that I hated my job, but had no idea what to do or where to go next. The thought of starting on the recruitment treadmill filled me with dread. I knew I didn't want to be a consultant any more, but I didn't have a clue about what I did want to do.

Looking back, I see that the redundancy was the best thing that could ever have happened to me. It forced me to come out of denial and stop putting up with a job that I hated. A month later, I had a business idea that filled me with such excitement and enthusiasm that I couldn't imagine doing anything else.

I have learned that out of misery can come great happiness. It probably took things to get that bad for me to even consider starting my own business. Pain is a great motivator. So don't worry if you hit that void, when you have no idea where life is going to take you next or how you're going to pay the bills. That's sometimes exactly the right environment you need to motivate you to take the really big leap that you've been avoiding for years.

Baby step 1:
The boiled-frog syndrome

There is a fact about frogs that isn't particularly pleasant. I don't actually want to know how this was discovered, but if you put a frog in water and let the water slowly heat up, the frog will become so soporific that it doesn't jump out, but slowly boils to death. However, if you were to put a frog in hot water, it would jump out immediately.

It's the same for humans. Life can get really 'hot' and uncomfortable without us really noticing or acknowledging it. Gradually, it gets worse and worse until our energy is completely drained and we no longer have the stamina to jump out of our situation. Pain is usually our warning system; when we feel pain, we take action to avoid it. But if the water gets hot slowly, we are lulled into a false sense of security. We get used to the heat, and may even begin to enjoy it. Then just as it's getting a bit too hot, we are so woozy we can't stir ourselves to action.

We can all get used to living with a constant feeling of malcontent. How many times have you left behind a difficult situation – by changing jobs, leaving your partner, moving away from a home with neighbours from hell, or simply going on holiday – only to suddenly recognize what you have been tolerating. It's only then that you can look back and wonder, 'How did I ever stand it?'

But we do stand it, because when we're in it, we think it's normal. We don't feel like we have a choice. We feel as if we just have to put up with it. It's a passive state. We're so sluggish that if feels like only an act of God or a gargantuan effort would change things – and in the end, to be honest, we just can't be bothered!

Anne Thorn, Big Leaping from lonely singledom to a vibrant social life

Being a single mum, I'd poured a lot of my time and energy into my son. When he left to go to university, I didn't know what to do with myself. I found myself being a 'helicopter mum' to poor old Toby, rushing up every week to see if he was okay at college. At home, I would find myself night after night watching some awful rubbish on TV and was desperate to go out, but had no friends in the area. I had this dreadful feeling of 'Is this it? Is this all I have to look forward to for the next 20 years?' But I didn't know what to do to change it.

10 ways to tell if you're about to be boiled to death

1. You wake up every morning and switch the snooze button on at least five times.
2. You tell someone about your life situation and they react in a shocked or horrified way and say things like, 'You don't have to stand for this.'
3. You daydream about your situation coming to an end by an act of God – a car accident, a fire or a tornado (that will whisk you off to the Land of Oz, of course).

4. You sleep, watch television or drink – a lot.

5. You avoid having conversations about your situation with 'motivated' friends, relatives or colleagues. They don't really understand what it's like and and they'll just 'go on' at you.

6. You hang around with other people who are slowly boiling to death, swapping survival skills, saying things like, 'It's warm in here, isn't it?' To which you reply, 'Yeah, but if you keep moving from foot to foot, it's not so bad.'

7. You blame other people – usually one particular person – for what is happening to you, and can talk about this person endlessly, e.g. how they are impossible to work for/live with, etc.

8. You feel powerless to change the situation.

9. You drive very fast at inappropriate moments or sleep with inappropriate people or put your life at risk on a weekly basis (see point 3).

10. You have to deal with niggling health problems frequently, such as back pain, skin problems, weight issues or lack of energy.

 Jules Ritter, Big Leaping from mother and housewife to writer and journalist

Before I started coaching, I was the princess in the castle on the hill looking out of the window, surrounded by beautiful scenery, feeling bored. I am the sort of person who sticks to commitments and tries very hard to do my best at whatever I am doing.

Thus I was a good wife and mother to my three children, married to a successful man with his own company, who worked 12–15 hour days, which meant no room for me to work as I was effectively replacing him. Which was fine, as the benefits were plenty and we had a lovely life. But this was part of the problem: how could I be bored? Why? I already had so much, why did I want more? But my true essence was restless. I had had an exciting career before my marriage, working at the UN, and then for an advertising agency in Dubai, and I missed it.

When the children were little, it worked fine. I was all too happy to play Barbie at home, and would flop into bed contented and happy at the end of each day. But as they got older and more independent, with their own interests, spending hours away from home and me, I started to find I had whole afternoons free and I didn't know what to do with myself. When my son started making university choices and running for the exit, I got overly sentimental about the whole thing, crying impulsively and boring my friends silly with my empty-nest syndrome.

I found myself saying to my husband things like, 'It's okay for you, you have a career, a reputation, a life outside this family,' when he started complaining about the long hours he had to work. I kept thinking that my husband, whom I had met when I was 21 years old, and I would just continue as we were, chugging along in our lovely, safe, elegant lives and probably die together on the same night in bed holding hands, but rather than feeling how lovely this would be, a voice in my head kept shrieking BORING!!!

I was stuck in my boiled-frog syndrome, but didn't know what I wanted to do. I felt aimless, drifting. Something had to change.

How to get out of the pan without boiling to death

The boiled-frog syndrome is probably one of the most dangerous states to be in. It can go on for years. To make the Big Leap, the first leap you have to make is out of the warm water. So let's turn up the heat so you can jump out. Ready to leap?

Ready
to leap **?**

Exercise: LEAP OUT OF DENIAL

It's not popular to be downbeat. 'Actually my life is crap,' would probably not go down well at your school reunion. But in this exercise, I want you to focus on the simple, unadorned truth. It's time to look yourself in the eye and get brutally honest about your life. It's time to get out of the pan of warm water and out of denial. Answer the following questions in your Big Leap journal.

- What is currently making you unhappy?
- Where are you betraying yourself right now?
- Where are you playing small in your life?
- What has been the lowest point in the last month? Describe that point in detail. How did it make you feel about yourself?
- What do you have to believe about yourself to create this situation in your life?
- What is the thing you are most afraid to say out loud about your life?
- What are you scared is happening to you?
- If you were run over by a bus tomorrow, what would be your greatest regret?

Okay. Are you depressed yet? If you think that was hard, brace yourself. Because now comes the really tricky bit. I want you to read your answers to a witness. I want you to stand up and be counted, to come out of denial and say how you feel about your life – out loud!

A word of warning here. Make sure you choose your witness carefully. Your witness has to be someone who loves you, who is unconditionally supportive. Only do this with your best friends and fans. And even with them, coach them to hear your statement supportively. Ask them to simply listen. Tell them that no advice is needed, nor any comments. Your words simply need to be heard in a non-judgmental space. You could perhaps ask them to applaud you after you've finished – if that doesn't seem too touchy-feely – applaud you for your bravery, because you've just made a big step. The first step is often the hardest, and this is a tough one: stating why you're unhappy, but not quite knowing where to go next. It's official, you've just stepped out of your comfort zone. Are you feeling sick yet?

Rachel Dobson, Big Leaping from Sunday tabloid journalist to freelance journalist and property developer

'Leaping out of denial' was my first piece of homework. I was constantly thinking about it, but putting off looking at it.

When eventually I did get down to business, I couldn't stop crying. How the hell did I end up so despairing? I'd set out to do my dream job of journalist. I worked with a great team of people and had a good track record. But I abhorred the work I did. I didn't want to write picture captions describing Geri Halliwell's 'fabulous' weight loss when I knew she had an eating disorder.

I felt I only had myself to blame for ending up in such a situation. I thought of my job as an endurance test. But I believed that to earn the money that I made, you had to put up with it.

The 'lowest point of the month' was the toughest question. How to choose from so many daily occurrences? I remember wishing an injury on myself – a broken leg would have done nicely – just so I could take time off the merry-go-round of work. What must I believe about myself to put up with my work situation day in, day out? When I realized, I thought I must be crackers. I would never expect anyone else to put up with that kind of environment.

In the end, I turned on myself, was angry at allowing this to happen – after all, nobody else had done this to me. But that's a good thing in a way. I got myself into this situation, and so I could get myself out. You complete an exercise like this and plummet to the depths of despair, but in a way it's good because you see that ultimately you are responsible for your own life. It's just up to us to make the changes. Painful as it may be to see the truth in black and white, it's also incredibly motivating.

Baby step 2:
Victim City

Rachel makes a good point. When we come out of denial, it's not particularly pleasant. It's always good to be able to blame someone else for your misfortunes; perhaps it's the parents who never gave us the love we needed, the so-called friends who never supported us, the boss that bullied us, the wife who spent all our money, the boyfriend who broke our heart, *yada, yada, yada* …

Undoubtedly, life can feel very tough at times. But living in Victim City keeps us stuck. It also keeps us safe. After all, you can blame everyone else for your crap life – your parents, your stressful job, your fascist boss. You can tell yourself it's not your fault. It's out of your control. You can moan and grumble, but you don't have to do anything about it. You can keep your pride intact about how stressed and miserable you are and remain a martyr to the cause.

'Oh, stop being a victim and start getting a life,' said my coach in my very first session. Get a life? I didn't even know what that meant. Up until that point, life had happened to me. Then, there I was in my first session being asked to take responsibility, to be the creator of my life rather than the victim of it. It scared the hell out of me.

Because it is scary, you're allowed to say, 'But it's not fair, it's not my fault, they did it to me, I couldn't do anything about it!' Life can be hard sometimes and can deal us some tough blows, but even if we can't change what happened or is happening, we can change what we think about it.

Don't misunderstand me. This is not about blaming yourself. This is not about flagellating yourself about what a stupid/weak/sad person you must be to put up with this. It is about becoming self-aware enough to recognize certain behaviours you may have that always seem to attract the same kind of heartbreaking men/has you battling with the boss in every job/has you working 16 hours a day when your colleagues work 8 hours.

To make the Big Leap journey, you need to discover that you don't have to be on a mission to change the world: just on a mission to change yourself, or rather your thinking. Whenever you find yourself squirming in your seat and pointing a finger at whoever is ruining your life at that particular moment, take a deep breath, and then take responsibility for it and put the focus back on to what you can think or do differently to change things.

If I'm honest, I resist doing this as much as the next person. When I'm in a full-scale argument, I admit that I don't calmly sit down and think to myself, 'What can I think or do differently here?' I'm too busy jumping up and down and frothing at the mouth. But several years into my Big Leap journey, I know that I can't get away with blaming it all on someone else – at least not for very long. Eventually, I realize that I have to take responsibility, and until I stop frothing and start working out my role in the proceedings, then I get nowhere fast.

So how do you make the journey out of Victim City? Why, make the Big Leap, of course.

Ready to leap

Exercise: MAKE THE BIG LEAP

A Big Leap is a radical shift into BIG thinking – expansive, loving, wise thinking – that challenges one or more of the assumptions you have previously made about life. Answer the following questions in your Big Leap journal.

- What are the little thoughts and stories that keep you stuck in Victim City? (S/he did that to me. S/he doesn't like me. They are out to get me.)
- How do these thoughts help or serve you? (e.g. Do they keep you safe in your comfort zone?)
- What do these little thoughts cost you? (e.g. Do they make you miserable and cost you your health and happiness/goals?)
- If you were going to make a leap and tell a different and BIG story, where you come from your expanded, forgiving and empowered place, what would it be? (I can achieve anything when I put my mind to it. I'm lovely and this is their problem, not mine. I will find a way through this. This too shall pass.)

Yes, I know this is a leap. The good news is that the more successfully you are able to make this shift in thinking, the more you are actually reprogramming your brain to set this as your default setting.

I've written a book about this called *The Big Peace*, which is a 90-day programme to train the brain to make the Big Leap from little thoughts to big thoughts that make you more content, happier and healthier. Here, I will explain briefly how it works.

There is a new pioneering science called neuroplasticity, which has revealed that the brain can change its childhood emotional and genetic 'programming', altering its actual physical circuitry, if we think different thoughts and take different actions.

Decades of scientific research and dogma that told us the brain was fixed in form and function have been overturned. It turns out that our brains are like gardens, and our neural pathways blossom the more time we spend tending them – be it practising a violin, which expands the part of the brain that controls the fingers, or restoring mental health by thinking thoughts in a different way. Conversely, it has been found that if we don't take control of our thoughts and actions, weeds of negative and destructive thinking and behaviour can easily take over.

The good news is that scientists now say that, with consistent tending, we can vastly improve our 'set point' of happiness and peace of mind. It's what the personal development industry has been saying for years, but now there is scientific credibility to back it up. We do not have to be victims of our upbringing or even our genetics – we can change our lives by thinking and acting differently.

But there is some bad news. Changing our way of thinking is not always easy. Unfortunately, we are programmed physiologically to think little thoughts rather than big thoughts. It's part of our survival wiring. Little thoughts such as fear, anger and greed are triggered in what is known as the 'reptilian' brain. This is a very ancient part of the brain that is hardwired to react to danger or threat. Its key role is to broadcast messages to protect us from harm. It had a vital role to play in prehistoric times, in situations when 'fight or flight' meant just that: with lions and tigers and bears on the loose.

In contemporary society, however, where social conflicts are more likely to occur than encounters with predators, a harmless but emotionally charged situation can trigger uncontrollable fear or anger, leading to arguments and stress. We can find ourselves lying in bed worrying over some imaginary threat and left with a nameless anxiety that has nowhere to go and leaves us tearing the sheets with our teeth, wringing our hands and doing the headless-chicken dance – fearful, but doing nothing. Not good.

I will be giving you tools to make the Big Leap from little thoughts to big thoughts, but for now, I'd like to introduce you to someone.

Baby step 3:
Meet your Inner Pessimist

Now I'd like you to personify that reptilian part of your brain and give it a name. I call it your 'Inner Pessimist', and you're probably very well acquainted with him* already. The Inner Pessimist is always there, at every crossroads in life, hovering in the wings: you've decided to leave your career and company car behind to explore India, or you've decided to leave your diaphragm in the cupboard to try for a baby, or you've decided to leave your wife and home to discover yourself. In any of these cases, you're leaving struggle behind in the search of a delightful life; you're leaving the warmth and safety of what you know to start something new. You're scared, but you're going to try anyway. But then the Inner Pessimist says, 'Oh, you don't wanna be doing that!' 'What have I got to lose?' you respond. 'Everything!' shouts your Inner Pessimist.

*My Inner Pessimist is male and as such I refer to the Inner Pessimist as 'he' throughout this book. Yours may well be female, though, so feel free to call your Inner Pessimist 'she'.

If only our Inner Pessimist lived in the real world. Then we could tell him to mind his own business. But the Inner Pessimist I'm talking about doesn't live on your street; he lives in your head.

When you're considering coming out of denial, you're in a very vulnerable position. You need lots of soothing encouragement, handholding and acknowledgement. Your Inner Pessimist knows this and is ready to pounce. He will say, 'I'm just being realistic ...' Don't be fooled – your Inner Pessimist is ready to dismiss, negate and pour scorn on every one of your ideas and dreams.

10 things your Inner Pessimist is likely to say

1. You're not good enough. I'd shelve this idea if I were you.
2. You're a loser. Good try, but it's best to quit while you're ahead.
3. You're really stupid! Whatever you do, don't open your mouth.
4. Really they all despise you and laugh at you behind your back. I'd stay in if I were you.
5. You're fat, your nose is huge and you're funny-looking. They would never fancy you in a month of Sundays, so don't make a fool of yourself.
6. You're talentless. Don't show anyone your work or you'll just humiliate yourself.
7. They're rich and posh, and you're common and poor. Never the twain shall meet.
8. You might have hit a lucky streak, but it will all go wrong soon. I wouldn't celebrate if I were you.
9. You're poor, you're stupid and you're ugly – and you're thinking about doing what?! Oh, don't make me laugh ...
10. You life is terrible because you are terrible.

Many of us live our lives thinking that our Inner Pessimist is the voice of truth because of the huge, starring role he plays in our head. The Inner Pessimist shouts so loudly that we don't think there is an alternative. The good news is, there is, but we're going to find out about that in Big Leap Step 3. For now, I don't want you to fight your Inner Pessimist; I simply want you to be aware of him. Learn to recognize that voice, its style and its script, and how you feel in your body when your Inner Pessimist is in charge.

Ready to leap

Exercise: GETTING THE MEASURE OF YOUR INNER PESSIMIST

Answer the following in your journal.

1. Give your Inner Pessimist a name and a character. Write a description of him/her. Does he have dyed hair, an orange tan and a thin-lipped smile? Go to town and really flesh him out. How does he speak? In a dull monotone or in a vicious rant?

2. You're probably already very familiar with the script that your Inner Pessimist generally uses. Think about this script and answer the following questions.

- What is the pessimistic script that keeps me frozen in fear? (Be specific – write the script out in great detail.)
- How does that script serve me? (e.g. 'It allows me to torture myself so I keep myself small, which means I don't have to move out of my comfort zone, make a commitment to anything new or risk getting hurt.')
- What does it cost me? (e.g. 'I feel unbearably miserable. It costs me true peace of mind.')
- When your Inner Pessimist is in charge, how do you feel physically? Exhausted? Wired? (I get a pain between my shoulder blades and I can't smile properly – my lips stick to my teeth if I try.)

Learn to love your Inner Pessimist

Let's have some compassion for the Inner Pessimist.
Difficult, I admit, when he's swearing at us and calling us
names, but we need to understand that the Inner
Pessimist is just very, very scared. I don't want you to
fight him. (He'll always win.) At this stage in the game,
I simply want you to be aware of him. Try this
visualization exercise.

Exercise: SHRINKING AND COMFORTING YOUR INNER PESSIMIST

Ready **?**
to leap

Imagine your Inner Pessimist as a little boy or girl – a
child of around 6 to 8 years old. Imagine that you are
seeing the world and life through this 6 year old's eyes.
What is your Inner Pessimist afraid of?

Rather than fighting with, chastising or sending this child
to their room, imagine you are comforting them. Give
that child the comfort and love and encouragement they
need to stop being afraid and to feel safe again.

Imagine the adult you comforting that child. What do
you say? How do you say it? I know this may sound
crazy, but try it.

Your Inner Pessimist is scared. Scared witless. If you're
going to change your life and leap out of the Big Blah, it's
much easier to calm down your Inner Pessimist first. Stop
ignoring him. Stop putting your fingers in your ears and
start reassuring him. You'll be amazed at what happens
when you do. Imagine looking your little Inner Pessimist
right in the eye and offering plenty of hugs and comfort
until he stops being afraid.

This visualization works because when you comfort your Inner Pessimist, you are lighting up a different part of your brain to the reptilian brain. But more of that in Big Leap Step 3. For now, know that showing compassion and love for yourself gets you operating from what I call your Big Peace place. According to medical psychologists, it's physiologically impossible for your mind to be scared while at the same time generating love and compassion. So far, so good. In Big Leap Step One, the main goal is to come out of denial and get prepared to leap. But normally, the leap itself comes when a catalyst hits your life – be it good or bad – losing your job, deciding to emigrate, falling ill or falling in love. Brace yourself for the wake-up call.

Your Inner Pessimist is probably saying right now ...

'Big Leap? More like a Big Heap! Don't listen to any more of this drivel. Put the book down and go watch your favourite TV programme instead. This author is obviously insane. It's not denial at all. It's simply reality. That's just how life is. And I don't want any hugs or compassion thank you very much. Keep your hands to yourself! I think it's better for everyone if you put this book down now. Whatever you do, don't turn the page.'

What you need to be doing right now ...

Thank your Inner Pessimist for this contribution, give him a blanket, and then turn the page.

The Big Wake-up Call

'It's a twister, it's a twister!'

'The ultimate measure of a man is not where he stands in moments of comfort and convenience, but where he stands at times of challenge and controversy.'

– MARTIN LUTHER KING, JR, CIVIL RIGHTS LEADER (1929–68)

Big Leap Step 2:   **THE BABY STEPS**

1. Feeling everything
2. Getting your needs met
3. The void of fear

You can be going along quite happily (or unhappily) in life, and then, suddenly, bang! There is an 'invitation' to grow, change, move on, move out. In movies, it's called the catalyst moment: when the hero falls in love, falls down a hole, decides to go rescue the princess, her kid and the dog. In life, I call it the Big Wake-up Call. It is often jarring and threatens your comfort zone. Even if you've been bitching about your old life/your boss/your partner, when you get the call, you'd often do anything rather than answer it. I've had several wake-up calls in my life, and I always, always resist it – even if the change seems to be good. I take comfort that even Luke Skywalker, one of my all-time favourite heroes, dragged his heels before agreeing to fight the Empire and rescue Princess Leia. So don't worry, if you find yourself pretending you didn't quite hear what your boss said, or you think it's jam on your husband's shirt collar, it's normal. It's just another version of denial before you're ready to face the big changes ahead.

What you're probably thinking at Big Leap Step 2

- Oh shit.
- Excuse me, can you repeat that?
- This cannot be happening to me.
- This is like a dream come true!
- If I whistle loudly enough, I won't hear what they're saying.
- I'm in love/screwed/in big trouble.
- What am I going to do with all this money/without any money?

What you're probably doing at Big Leap Step 2

- Staring into space.
- Screaming hysterically.
- Ringing all your friends and crying.
- Ringing all your friends and laughing (then crying).
- Clinging to your dog/partner/anything that seems familiar and laughing and/or crying.

In Big Leap Step One, you've come out of denial and acknowledged that something might have to change. At this point, you might not be that keen on changing anything. Your Inner Pessimist is jumping up and down, having a tantrum and telling you to get realistic. The Inner Pessimist doesn't like change. Unfortunately, the Big Leap process is essentially about change. So expect your Inner Pessimist as a constant companion on this journey.

In this step of the process, a catalyst makes you realize that something has to change because you can't stay in limbo any more. A wake-up call isn't necessarily a bad thing. It can be great. You may have been promoted or received/ made a marriage proposal; you may have won a contract or a large sum of money. Or it might not be so great.

Irene Brankin, psychologist and coach. Big Leaping from illness to launching a business and writing a book

My Wake-up Call was that I nearly died. When I was diagnosed with bowel cancer in my 60s, they operated and gave me chemotherapy, which was too strong and burst my colon. I got septicaemia and was in intensive care. It took me two years to recover. It was another wake-up call – at my age, I've had a few! But this time, I wanted to shake everyone and say, 'For God's sake, get on with your life – live! This is your one shot. Don't waste it.'

I see so many women with massive potential living half-lives. They may be smiling, but their energy and life is gone. I realized that I wanted to give these women a voice and a map to getting their groove back. At 30, I was a mother and homemaker. I retrained over seven years to become a psychotherapist. That Big Leap was born out of thinking that there has to be more to life. Now, aged 65 and having faced death, I want to tell the world what I've learned and help others to find fulfilment.

What's your Wake-up Call?

- You realize it isn't jam on your partner's collar.
- Your partner's lover sends you a text.
- Your loved one proposes.
- You lose your job.
- You get a new job.
- You resign from your job.
- You are facing a health crisis.
- A loved one is facing a health crisis.
- Someone crashes into your car.
- Your business goes bust.
- You win the lottery.
- Someone you love dies.

Baby step 1:
Feeling everything

Everyone's reaction to the Wake-up Call is different. You will probably go through a whole range of emotions, all of which are completely normal. Don't be surprised if you feel any or all of these emotions:

Numb

You literally feel nothing – no excitement, no despair. People are constantly quizzing you about how you feel and look perplexed when you say, 'I'm absolutely fine.' Because you are: you can't feel anything.

Confusion

When change happens, we may have to let go of a role we've been playing or a sense of our identity that we have taken on. When we challenge or let go of that perception of ourselves, we can feel confused because 'We don't know who we are any more.' You were perhaps defined by a role – mother/lover/rich man/poor woman/healthy/sick. 'This is who I was in the world,' you have told yourself over and over again. You took on the role of 'happily married' or 'ambitious bread-winner', and when that role changes, you think, 'Well, who am I now?'

Grief

Sometimes the Wake-up Call comes with a great loss. You lose your partner, your health, or a way of life that you loved, and the grief is intense as you desperately try to hold on to a life that is lost to you now. You weep for a lost era, and at times, it feels unbearable.

Anger and rage

With grief can come pockets of anger and rage, as you shake your fist at the gods or the establishment, an ex-partner or the unfairness of it all. 'Why me?' you scream. 'It's just not fair.' You wallow in feelings of bitterness and fantasize about revenge.

Exhilaration

'I can do this, I can do this, I can do this,' you repeat. You feel high and experience a surge of strength and resolve as you start to research and work out ways to make a new life happen. The world is your oyster, you think.

 Marc Lockley, Big Leaping from Head of Agency Sales to business owner, author and online columnist

I kept daydreaming of a different kind of life, but every time I did, I heard this voice, 'Oh, come on, get real. You're never going to leave this job. You haven't got a degree, you haven't got a trade, you're not a doctor or a lawyer. You've winged it for years.' But at the end of the day, you can listen to that voice and live in fear, or just go for it. In the end, you just have to leap. I bit the bullet and resigned. Everyone thought that I'd gone mad. I did have a moment of thinking, 'What the hell have I done?' Then I went numb. No euphoria, nothing. But deep down, I knew that I needed and wanted to leave.

This too shall pass

When you're feeling all of these emotions, you may begin to panic. Often we stay in the blah zone for exactly that reason – so we don't have to feel these feelings. When powerful emotions erupt to the surface, you may try to do anything, anything, anything rather than feel them.

But feeling these emotions is part of the Big Leap journey. The only way out is to go through.

One of the most astonishing discoveries I have made in the past couple of years is that I don't always have to aspire to being happy. Living a big life doesn't always mean you're living a happy one. In fact, I realized that one of my major obstacles was my belief that life 'should' be happy, good, pleasant and enjoyable all the time. Queen of positive thinking, mantras and affirmations, I had been trained to reframe my thoughts and experiences so that I could feel good whenever I wanted. But you know what? This didn't make me feel happy. It made me feel that it was wrong if, underneath, I really felt irritated, sad, mad or miserable. My thought process went like this, 'I'm irritated/sad/mad/miserable, so I'm not doing life right. Quick, what can I do to change how I feel?' That becomes exhausting.

For me, living my big life now means surrendering to both the sorrowful and happy points in my day, knowing it's OK to feel a whole rainbow of emotions – irritation, sadness, anger, happiness, amusement – sometimes all within five minutes. These feelings pass through like waves – be it intense love while watching my son sleep or irritation with him when he refuses to get out of the car while smearing his chocolate-coated hands on the window.

You may be feeling very confused at this stage, but let 'This too shall pass' be your mantra. Accept what you feel in any given moment and don't start building up great big stories in your head about it. Don't put a magnifying glass over it. Just observe the feeling, identify it and then let it float away. This too shall pass.

This does take practice.

Ready
to leap

Exercise: FEEL YOUR FEELINGS

Sit where you won't be disturbed for 10 minutes and try these steps. Practise every day.

- Start to observe your thoughts/feelings and write them down as you notice them. How do you experience them? Is it like a voice in your head? A constant dialogue? Or are you more aware of how you feel? Where do you feel your feelings? In one place – your heart? Your throat? Or in lots of places?
- Pay attention when you get caught up with a thought or a feeling and notice what happens to your body.
- Keep repeating 'This too shall pass' and notice what happens to the thought or feeling. Don't try to push it away or resist it – simply observe what happens.
- Ask yourself the question, if you are not present in your thoughts or feelings, who are you? Who is doing the observing?

Andrew Stone, Big Leaping from journalist on a trade magazine to globetrotting as a travel-guide writer

I was 29 and working for a London publishing trade magazine. I got the chance to go out to some party or other every night, so the job was essentially great for a bloke in his twenties. Everything else in my life looked set, too. I was in a serious relationship with a girlfriend I loved and I had bought a flat. But I looked into the future of married life, kids, a steady desk job, and I just knew I didn't want that – not yet, anyway. I wanted to travel, I wanted adventure. But try telling that to your parents or to your friends who value security more than you do. They thought I was insane.

Working with my coach, I literally picked a city – Hong Kong – and decided I was going to go there on such-and-such a date. I planned my resignation. The coaching helped me identify that travel-guide writing would be the ideal profession for me, but at that point I was more intent on just making the leap. Just resigning and getting on a plane was a great way of making sure I made the leap. You then have no choice but to make your new life work.

And I had my work cut out. I arrived in Hong Kong with hardly any savings in the bank and no firm work lined up. If someone had told me what my first year would be like, I probably would have been too scared to do it. That first year became a lesson in how little you can actually live on. On £7,000 I managed to travel to China twice, as well as Cambodia and Africa. Although I never seemed to have any money, I never once woke up dreading the day ahead.

If you're having trouble motivating yourself to make the leap out of your old life, set it up that not to do it is more painful than actually doing it. I told everyone what I was going to do, set a date to fly off, set a date to resign and set up business meetings for when I got there. If I had bottled it, I would have felt very foolish. I know it's a cliché, but sometimes you have to 'just do it'. Leap now and worry later, I say.

Baby step 2:
Getting your needs met

Another reason why the wake-up call can be very painful is that it often changes the way your emotional needs are met. If you suddenly lose your job and the need to be respected that was tied up in your role is no longer being met, you will feel very unhappy. If you have a need for freedom and your partner suddenly proposes, you may react in a way that no one expects.

Emotional needs – for approval, security, control or acclaim – when met, can make you feel satisfied, content, peaceful, at one with the world. When they are not met, you go into meltdown. Often you cannot get on with creating positive changes until they are met, because the pain of unmet needs will always win over what you 'want'. Having unmet needs feels like being permanently hungry. They make you irritable and snappy, and if they go on long enough, they can make you feel as if you are emotionally starving.

It is much easier to make the Big Leap when you're working on a metaphorical full stomach; otherwise you waste a lot of energy scouring the world for leftovers. Sometimes, if you're starving for your need to be met, you end up down blind alleys, rifling through bins for scraps. You definitely need to know what your emotional needs are if your Big Leap journey is going to be a pleasant and successful one.

Emotional needs, however, are not a popular concept in Western society. The word 'needy' is usually spat out as an insult – the more 'needless' you appear, the more emotionally healthy you are perceived to be. That's a dangerous concept to buy into, because unless you're some kind of enlightened being, you will have emotional needs. Deny them and they become like hidden addictions. You will do anything to get your fix.

Our unmet childhood needs snap at our heels waiting to be fed, getting more and more irritated and upset as we stick our heads in the sand and ignore them. For most of us, denying our needs may simply be a result of being unaware of them.

Whether you work 16 hours a day to meet your need to be accepted by your boss, or you eat maggots on a trashy TV show to meet your need for acclaim, you should never underestimate the depths of miserable or bizarre behaviour you can sink to when trying to get your emotional needs met. Behind practically every addiction is an unmet need. If you find yourself overeating, smoking or drinking, you are most likely trying to anaesthetize the pain of your unmet needs.

One of the reasons why many of us find it difficult to stop our bad habits has nothing to do with the addictive quality of the substance itself, but everything to do with trying to avoid feeling the pain of an unmet need. It is kinder to yourself (and easier) to get your needs met before trying to give up a bad habit.

The needs-fulfilment process probably causes more resistance than any exercise in the Big Leap, so if you want to throw the book across the room after reading this bit, that's okay. You are even allowed to skip it, if you wish. Though if you do, you will discover in Big Leap Step 5 what happens if we listen to our Inner Pessimist and don't attend to our unmet needs.

Marc Lockley, Big Leaping from Head of Agency Sales to business owner, author and online columnist

I realize now that the big job I had at a major national newspaper met my need to be successful. It's a need that had to be met for me to feel content. Today, I get that need met in a healthier way. Rather than work 60 hours a week and be away from my family with no work–life balance, I've set up a coaching practice, written a book, and write a column for a national newspaper about something I'm passionate about. Bingo! I'm meeting my need to be successful, but doing it sitting in the garden, writing in the sunshine.

Ready to leap

Exercise: IDENTIFY AND MEET YOUR NEEDS

If you are not clear about your needs, look at the following statements and see if a pattern emerges that will help you identify your unmet need. There are hundreds of different needs, but there are some common groups.

1. **Do you answer 'yes' to three or more of these statements?**

   - I become tense when someone is late.
   - I become annoyed by others' sloppy standards.
   - I am a tidy and methodical person.
   - I can get snappy with disorganized people.
   - I like to have possession of the remote control.

   Possible unmet need: To be right; to be perfect

2. **Do you answer 'yes' to three or more of these statements?**

   - I'm always exhausted because I tend to rush around helping out my friends.
   - I know instinctively how to make people feel good.
   - I make a big effort to find out what is going on in the lives of friends and family so I can be there for them.
   - I feel outraged and resentful if people don't appreciate me.
   - I send thoughtful presents and cards to friends and colleagues just to let them know I'm thinking of them.

   Possible unmet need: To be approved of; to be needed; to be loved; to be cherished; to be liked

3. **Do you answer 'yes' to three or more of these statements?**

- When things are going well for me, I literally light up inside.
- I work very long hours to ensure something is a success.
- I'd rather die than be a failure.
- I'm really aware of how friends and colleagues are doing and can be quite competitive.
- I am great at achieving goals.
- I have workaholic tendencies – I feel tense inside if I'm not accomplishing what I set out to do.

   Possible unmet need: To achieve; to be successful; to feel worthwhile; to be accepted

4. **Do you answer 'yes' to three or more of these statements?**

- If I'm criticized or misunderstood, I sulk.
- People say I can be difficult and too emotional, but what's wrong with that?
- I know how to make a really big scene if I don't get what I want.
- Rules are meant to be broken.
- I tend to brood a lot about my negative feelings.

   Possible unmet need: For acclaim; to be special; to be different; to be heard; to be understood

5. **Do you answer 'yes' to three or more of these statements?**

-   I'm an expert in my area.
-   I love to study something in depth and really get my teeth stuck into it.
-   I am the eternal student.
-   I often lose track of time because I get carried away with what I'm doing.
-   I won't try something new until I'm confident that I know everything I need to know.

    Possible unmet need: To be competent; to be the expert; to be capable

6. **Do you answer 'yes' to three or more of these statements?**

-   Anxiety is my middle name.
-   I worry about everything, everybody and his dog.
-   I like having a boss I can respect.
-   I find it difficult to make a decision without asking all my friends, my parents and my colleagues first.
-   It takes me ages to change jobs.

    Possible unmet need: For security; for safety; for support; for certainty

7. **Do you answer 'yes' to three or more of these statements?**

-   I get bored easily.
-   I'm curious about stuff.
-   I love travelling and having fabulous holidays.

- I am all over the place most of the time – people think I'm a bit dizzy.
- I always feel like I'm missing out on things – the grass is always greener on the other side.

Possible unmet need: To be stimulated; to be free; to be satisfied

8. **Do you answer 'yes' to three or more of these statements?**

- I like to challenge people. No one could call me a shrinking violet.
- I tend to have huge temper tantrums.
- I am independent and don't like people trying to tie me down.
- I don't rely on anyone.
- I love trying to achieve the impossible.

Possible unmet need: To protect yourself; to determine your own course in life

9. **Do you answer 'yes' to three or more of these statements?**

- I'm one of life's peacemakers – I can't bear a scene.
- There's no point dwelling on the negative – is there?
- I like my home comforts.
- Most people tend to get too worked up about the little things – what's the point?
- I go with the flow.

Possible unmet need: For calm; for agreement; for steadiness; for peace

Exercise: IDENTIFYING THE SOURCE OF YOUR UNMET NEEDS

As we have discussed, our unmet needs usually stem from childhood. So now, travel back in time and answer the following questions in your journal.

- As a child, what behaviour earned you rewards?
- What behaviour earned you disapproval?
- What decisions did you make as a child to survive and thrive in your family?
- How do those decisions show up in your life now?
- What effects are those decisions having on your life?
- What decisions could you now make differently to be able to survive and thrive as an adult?

Exercise: FULFILLING YOUR EMOTIONAL NEEDS

Now it's time to work out a strategy to get your needs fulfilled in a healthy, adult way. You will need help from others to do this. Choose people who love you enough to help you, so create your need-meeting team carefully. If you're struggling to think of a team, just choose one person.

- Choose a team of friends and/or family members who would be willing to help you meet your needs.
- Explain to them the concept of unmet needs.
- Choose the unmet need with the most symptoms; the one you recognize most easily.
- Create a 'need-fulfilment project' and give your team specific and measurable things to do or say to meet your need. For example, if you have a need for approval, get them to email you every day with another reason why they like or love you so much.

This exercise is very challenging. The problem with our unmet needs is that we assume people know what we need and are in some way choosing to withhold their love, support or praise. That's not the case – they simply don't know. (If they do know and they are withholding what you need, you should ask yourself why you are spending time with these people anyway.)

Asking others to meet your needs means risking confirmation that the Inner Pessimist is right – that it is unsafe, that you are unlovable unless you do a, b, or c, that love is conditional, that you must protect yourself or people will mock you. These are the hidden, and sometimes not so hidden, beliefs about ourselves that formed in childhood. We are going to tackle beliefs in Big Leap Step 4. For now, it's enough to identify your need-fulfilment team. Go on, try it.

Baby step 3:
The void of fear

Now that you have started feeling your feelings and begun to meet your emotional needs, the next baby step is to negotiate the void of fear. This is where you go when you've come out of denial, you've had your big wake-up call, and you decide that you're going to make some changes. But then you have one discouraging conversation or receive some unexpectedly negative information, and you simply give up and get trapped in the void of fear.

'I can't find what it is I want to do, nothing is inspiring me – I'll just stay with what I know,' you wail. Instead of moving forward, you teeter on the edge of possibility, but you hide from the light. After all, that brightness just makes the world seem even more terrifying than before. A whole new life is beckoning, but there are no guarantees, and there is no certainty. It simply feels like you're in a void, and if you don't fill it with faith and hope, it fills with fear instead.

 Lynne McNicoll, Big Leaping from housewife to running her own business and becoming a charity fundraiser

The void of fear was horrible for me. I knew something was wrong with my life, but I just felt I was stuck with it. I hadn't worked for seven or eight years, and knew I was withdrawing more and more, even from friends. I felt I wasn't even a good friend to be around. I was bored and boring. I hated myself for not doing anything about my boredom, my fitness, or being overweight.

My light at the end of the tunnel was an article I read in the Sunday Times *about coaching. That's when I thought, 'I should hire a coach.' Even then it took me weeks to call and start the process. I was scared of trying something and failing. What if I was crap at this as well as everything else I did?*

I felt I had a huge hand holding me back, telling me I was useless, telling me I deserved to be fat and bored. I was so ashamed of myself, I wouldn't go out with my partner to business events because I felt I looked awful and had no personality and would let him down. He never thought that and was so sad that I did.

I knew that if I started the coaching, my life would probably change, and I was scared of that, too. I knew I 'had' to change, to do something, but I was terrified. Committing to the coaching was a Big Leap for me. I was committing to myself, I was committing to change, I was committing to taking baby steps to a new life.

My advice for anyone trying to get out of the void of fear is to stop procrastinating and just do it! I hung around far too long there and it's agony. You can change your life; you're one baby step away!

The void of fear is where your Inner Pessimist is strongest. It's the only voice that you can hear. It can be all consuming: so huge, so paralyzing, it stops you in your tracks from doing anything. You can end up living in the limbo of the 'out of denial' phase, hating your life, feeling disappointed with yourself, but doing nothing to change it. It's a horrible place to live, and some people can spend their whole lives there.

What it feels like to live in the void of fear

- Hopeless: 'I'm stuck here.'
- Energy sapping: 'I can't be bothered.'
- Gut-churningly envious: 'Look at them with their perfect, smug lives …'
- Miserable: 'I hate my life, I hate my life, I hate my life.'
- Sad: 'I've wasted my life.'

Ann Norton, Big Leaping from Melbourne, Australia to London, England

When I arrived in London, the fear hit. Buying the plane ticket was easy, finding a flat was easy; it was handling the fear inside my head that was trickier.

Although I had a little financial cushion, I had to get a job fairly quickly. I started to lose my confidence after going into agencies and being turned down for admin jobs. At my last job, I used to handle budgets of over £1 million and was involved in award-winning programmes, and here I was being turned down for a typist's job. I started to fall back into that old belief that I wasn't good enough. If I'd allowed myself to spiral into the void of fear, I'm not sure I'd ever have got out.

With help from my coach, I would use affirmations every day to turn that belief around. My mantra was, 'I'll do the best I can and let go of the outcome.' For inspiration, I also created a 'vision board' of what I wanted. Baby step by baby step, I felt my confidence increase. I knew I would find a job that I loved, and eventually I did. But changing the way I felt made the journey a lot more pleasant.

Every day that we stay in the void of fear, it gets worse. All we can hear is our Inner Pessimist going on and on at us. It can be exhausting. We go back to the job or relationship that we know instinctively is wrong for us and try to make it right, trying hard to make it work. We come away feeling like we've been wrestling with a sabre-toothed tiger every day. It hasn't eaten you yet, but it might tomorrow.

The void of fear is also the place where envy loves to live. You look at other people with happy lives and are filled with a green, mean-spirited envy – you hate their clothes, their cars, even their happy children. You smile and nod over the garden wall, but secretly you want them to crash and burn – for him to lose his job, for her to get fat and ugly, for the kid to turn into a toad.

The void of fear is not a pleasant or pretty place to live. So put yourself out of your misery. Leave the void behind and make a decision.

Without knowing how you're going to achieve it or if it's right, make a decision that you are going to find a way to make the leap.

Anne Thorn, Big Leaping from lonely singledom to a vibrant social life

For our 50th birthdays, a girlfriend and I had promised we'd go on holiday together to celebrate. Then she met someone and bailed out on me, so I decided to go on my own. I was very brave and booked a tour to some Italian cities. I had an amazing time. I was so stimulated by the culture, by the sights. It was incredible. It was like a light coming on in my head and in my life. I knew that I wanted more of this feeling when I got home. I needed to make friends who I could go to the theatre with, or to the opera, or to visit beautiful cities. I wasn't quite sure how I was going to do it, but I just knew that life would never be the same after my visit to Venice. It was my wake-up call to what life had to offer.

Exercise: MAKE A DECISION

Ready to leap

Answer the following in your journal.

- What would it feel like to believe that there is another way of living, being, doing?
- What would it feel like if the Big Wake-up Call was a vehicle to start anew?
- What if this was a new beginning as well as an ending?
- What if somehow, some way you will find a way to survive and thrive in this new world?
- What if there was a way to let go of the past and embrace the future, right here, right now?
- What would that look and feel like?

This decision will light the way in the darkness. You will need that glimmer of hope and faith to be able to see your way forward. Darkness and misery can be scary, but they can also be great places to hide. When you light the match, you're scuppered, because then people can see where you are. You can't hide any longer. Are you willing to come out of hiding? Make that decision.

Your Inner Pessimist is probably saying right now ...

'Wake-up call? I'll give you a wake-up call. This is just a pile of crap. Don't listen to her. Life is hard, just accept it. That's how life is. There is no other way. If you ask anyone to help you with that needs-project thing, they're going to think you're weird. I think it's better for everyone if you put this book down now. Whatever you do, don't turn the page.'

What you need to be doing right now ...

Thank your Inner Pessimist for this contribution, give him a blanket to hide under, and turn the page anyway.

The Big New World

'We're not in Kansas anymore...'

'You can have anything you want if you want it desperately enough. You must want it with an inner exuberance that erupts through the skin and joins the energy that created the world.'

– SHEILA GRAHAM,
HOLLYWOOD COLUMNIST
(1904–88)

> **Big Leap Step 3:   THE BABY STEPS**
>
> 1. Welcome to la-la land
> 2. Meet your Inner Coach
> 3. The golden glow
> 4. The bingo moment
> 5. Create the vision
> 6. Setting goals in the present

Congratulations! You've taken your first steps and started your Big Leap adventure. This is where it starts to get interesting.

You've just landed in a new world that you can create anyway you want. Liberating, yes, but also a tad scary. This is where we start to explore your new world and what is possible. It is usually the fun and exhilarating bit.

What you're probably thinking at Big Leap Step 3

- Is it really possible to create what I want in my life?
- I'm scared, but I'm excited.
- This is just self-help psychobabble – it's not really possible to change.
- I don't know what I want.
- I can't have an extraordinary life because I'm not extraordinary.
- I want it all!
- I can have it all.
- Who am I kidding? I'll never escape this life.
- I'll never find 'the way' because I'm not clever enough.

What you're probably doing at Big Leap Step 3

- Going through the motions at work while logging on to the Internet to explore 'a few ideas'.
- Daydreaming of a different life when you're off-guard.
- Telling your best friend about a new idea you've had.
- Watching TV or reading books about people who have changed their lives.
- Writing a five-year plan.
- Spending the millions you are going to earn when you get to where you want to go.
- Laughing more – before being plunged into despair.
- Hiring a coach.

Big Leap Step 3 is where the birth of your dreams begins. Once the fog of denial has cleared and you are motivated to change, once you have started to get your unmet needs satisfied, you can now work out what it is you really want. Generally, we're all experts in knowing what we don't want, but identifying what we do want is sometimes much harder. We may glibly say, 'I want to win the lottery,' because we assume that money will make us happier (actually research proves the opposite, unless you're really poor to begin with). But after you've lain on a Caribbean beach for eight weeks and played with your new cars, clothes and accessories – what happens next?

If you've got a to-do list as long as your arm, you might be more clued up than some, but you still need to get from thought to action. If you haven't got a to-do list at all, then you probably need to find out what you want to put on it before you think about making your Big Leap. You may not have a clue as to what you want to do with your life. So let's go have some fun in la-la land.

Baby step 1:
Welcome to la-la land

La-la land? There are several names for this particular land mass. There's 'Cloud-cuckoo land', 'Get your head out of the clouds' continent, and 'She's off with the fairies again' island. Whatever yours is called, it's time to decide to take a trip to this strange and distant land, so leave reality behind and have some fun.

For once in your life, you don't have to 'get real' or listen to your Inner Pessimist, because you are simply going to daydream. When you daydream, your Inner Pessimist tends to go to sleep for a while because they don't feel threatened by flights of fancy. Visiting la-la land allows you to create your life exactly as you want it to be. You can be ostentatious and live it large in your dreams. You can dream outrageously!

What would your life look like if you really went to town? Try to see it, smell it – really go for imagining it.

There are only two rules: first, you must never wonder how you are going to do it for real; and second, anything goes – you can move to a different country or even fly to the moon, if you wish! But your vision of la-la land should make you laugh out loud, make you feel exhilarated and make you feel slightly bashful.

Exercise: DESCRIBE YOUR TRIP TO LA-LA LAND

Ready to leap **?**

Imagine that you are living your la-la land life. A journalist from a best-selling magazine is coming to interview you. Write your answers in your journal.

- Why does such a prestigious magazine want to interview you? What have you achieved?
- How will the journalist describe your lifestyle?
- How does the journalist describe you? What are you wearing? How old do you look?
- The journalist wants to know about your love life and family. How do you describe this?
- Paint a picture for the journalist of your average day.
- Describe the big highlight of the year for you. How did it make you feel?
- On your journey to achieving all you have in la-la land, you've had some 'crunch' moments. What decisions did you make that got you to this place?
- If you were to give one piece of advice to the magazine's readers, what would it be?
- The journalist asks you about your vision for the future. What is it?
- Tell the journalist what kind of legacy you would like to leave behind.

Nicky Hambleton-Jones, Big Leaping from management consultant to celebrity fashion stylist

In my la-la land, I am being interviewed by The Sunday Times Style *magazine because I front my own television series about NHJ Style, my styling company. The programme is spreading the message that you can transform yourself and raise your self-esteem by changing your look and your clothes.*

My big highlight this year is winning 'Businesswoman of the Year' for creating such a strong brand from nothing in such a short amount of time. I'm not just a dolly bird fronting a TV show, I'm known for my pioneering business brain.

The TV series has been a massive success, which helps promote my styling business and style academy. I spend three days a week working on my business and the other four with my gorgeous husband and two kids, one boy, one girl. We're all very healthy.

I'm looking particularly fetching today in just simple jeans and a white T-shirt with a toned-and-honed physique! Today we just got back from our villa in Tuscany where we generally spend six weeks of the year.

My husband interrupts the interview to kiss me and tell me our nanny, who helps out four days a week, has just arrived and he's going out; he asks to borrow my Audi TT parked outside our four-storey house in Clapham, London.

We're all very excited about next year when NHJ Style will hit New York. We are experimenting with a new line of accessories.

The legacy I want to leave behind? I want to be an inspiration to every woman out there with low self-esteem. I want to be seen as someone who has walked my talk – to show that you can live your dreams and you don't have to compromise.

I hate to admit it, but I've fooled you – because your la-la land vision is probably the nearest you'll get to how you really want your life to be. Without having to listen to your Inner Pessimist droning on about getting realistic, you can dream really big and not edit yourself. Nicky's la-la land vision is quite spooky even for me to read – and it is very inspiring. When she wrote this vision, she had moved out of her flat and was staying on friends' floors. She needed the income from renting her flat to survive financially because she had just been made redundant. Nicky was also single. She created this la-la land vision with her tongue firmly in her cheek.

More than a decade on, she's in the process of creating a global anti-ageing business after fronting her own TV series in the UK. She's also married, living in a four-storey house in Clapham with an Audi TT parked outside.

If she hadn't had the safe space of la-la land to dream in and had been asked to set some specific goals instead, I wonder if Nicky would have dreamed so big? Maybe. But her Inner Pessimist would also have leaped into action, screaming and shouting things like, 'Don't be ridiculous, you'll never achieve this in a month of Sundays.'

Baby step 2:
Meet your Inner Coach

To make the Big Leap, create the vision, and really attain all that we are capable of, we need to start listening to another voice. My clients have many different names for that voice, from the voice of reason to the voice of God, but I call it the Inner Coach. This is the Good Witch of the North moment. Your Inner Coach is your Inner Glinda – yes, with big sparkly frock and all.

Actually, the Inner Coach is the personification of love triggered in the part of the brain that I call the Big Peace place. Scientists have discovered that when we feel in the flow and are content and happy, we light up the left prefrontal lobe of the brain. This is the area of the brain that evolved later in human history than the reptilian brain of our Inner Pessimist. It is associated with happiness, creativity, the ability to understand right from wrong – and inner peace.

The bad news is that the way we are wired means our reptilian brain often dominates because, in evolutionary terms, it's important to be able to react to threats quickly. A state of inner peace may make us happier in the long run, but when we're being pursued by a lion, it's not going to be of much help. The structures in the primitive brain that trigger the flight-or-fight response are virtually automatic, while the ability to let go of fear and find a place of inner peace and calm is a much rarer state. And one we need to practise.

So in Big Leap Step 3, we are going to create a new character to practise with – your Inner Coach. The Big Peace personified. No matter what you call her, most of you will have heard her whispers. (Though she is so softly spoken, the whispers can be very difficult to hear.) I suspect she's the one that's been nudging you recently, telling you that there is another way, who perhaps even persuaded you to pick up this book. For you to make the Big Leap, it is her voice that you need to be able to tune into. She is the one who will champion your dreams; she is the one who will tell you to have faith when all seems dark; she is the one who will send help when the going gets tough.

10 things your Inner Coach is likely to say

1. You don't have to do anything to be loved.
2. You are smart, beautiful and funny.
3. Whatever happens, no matter how this turns out, you're going to be fine.
4. Oh, stop taking it all so seriously. In 12 months from now, you won't even remember what you were worrying about. Smile.
5. You have many gifts – when are you going to start using them?
6. Everyone doubts themselves; it's normal. Have faith. You're going to be okay.
7. What are you learning here?
8. Hold my hand, take a deep breath, and stop. You don't have to do anything to be accepted. Just be who you are.
9. When are you going to start having some fun?
10. Go on, I dare you, make the leap.

If we're really serious about hearing the wisdom of our Inner Coach, we need to learn to meditate. I won't bang on about it, but meditation – finding some quietness and being able to observe your thoughts for 5–15 minutes a day is the fast track for making the Big Leap. Our Inner Pessimist is so loud and strong and has ruled us for so long that it can take quite a bit of practise to hear the soft tones of the other voice. Meditation helps.

Firstly, it gives you space to gain an awareness of both voices. (I don't know about you, but when my Inner Pessimist gets all stoked up, I find it hard to separate his voice from reality. His voice and predictions become my world. Meditation helps me to start realizing that it's just one rather loud, aggressive voice.) And in the quiet, you can start hearing your Inner Coach, who has much nicer things to say.

Secondly, the Inner Coach speaks from a different place. While your Inner Pessimist speaks in your head – a rattling, obsessive drone that takes you round and round in circles, going nowhere – your Inner Coach speaks through your body, not through your thoughts. She talks through your gut instinct, your feelings and your intuition.

You cannot justify the messages of your Inner Coach through logic. You know you've heard her when you say, 'It's just a feeling you've got.' Or 'My gut feeling is telling me something.'

10 ways to tell when your Inner Coach is speaking to you

1. Your decision 'feels' right.
2. You 'just know' that this is the right path.
3. You are very clear about what you want.
4. You feel relaxed and happy about your decision.
5. You feel like you're in 'the flow'. Coincidences start happening. 'You'll never believe it …' is your favourite phrase.
6. You feel a flicker of excitement in your stomach.
7. You trust your inklings and intuition even though you have no evidence to back it up.
8. Even though life doesn't look like it's going in the right direction, you know it is.
9. You find yourself inspired with ideas more often than before.
10. You begin to trust your decisions.

Anne Thorn, Big Leaping from lonely singledom to a vibrant social life

I scanned the local papers and couldn't really find any groups I wanted to join, so with a bit of prompting from my coach, I decided to start one. Of course, my Inner Pessimist went mad. I got worried that no one would come, and if they did come, they'd be a bit strange or mad. But my Inner Coach calmed him down and told him that all I had to do was put an ad in the paper and just see what happened. So I did.

I put a free listing in the community events section of a directory distributed through the letterbox to homes in my area and e4friends.co.uk was born. I was really terrified that no one would respond, but the emails started rolling in. At our first meeting, 12 lovely ladies turned up. We now have 141 registered men and women and are growing each week.

It's really inspirational to see these people now meeting regularly, creating communities together, because I was brave enough to initiate the idea. It's all about listening to your Inner Coach. When you do that, not only do you change your life, you change the lives of others, too.

Exercise: HAVING TEA WITH YOUR INNER COACH

Ready to leap

Part 1

Imagine that you've invited your Inner Coach for tea and biscuits. What does she look like when she turns up? Does she have angel wings? Is she dressed in white or does she wear jeans? How does she speak? How do you know that she is speaking? How do you feel in your body when you hear her words?

Part 2

You're probably not very familiar with the script of your Inner Coach. The Inner Pessimist is such a bully that your Inner Coach usually gets drowned out. If she were to speak, what would she say? How do you know your Inner Coach is speaking to you?

If you're unfamiliar with her script, create one now in your journal. Be specific – write the script in great detail.

- When you're afraid, what does your Inner Coach say?
- When you feel you're not good enough, what does your Inner Coach say?
- When you feel ugly, what does your Inner Coach say?
- When you feel sad, what does your Inner Coach say?
- When you're tired, what does your Inner Coach say?
- What script would you have to hear to create the life you really want?

Keris Stainton, Big Leaping from an administration job to a full-time novelist

My Inner Pessimist (who seems to speak in the voice of various family members) is pretty much ever-present, but I'm learning to ignore it. When I started pitching freelance articles, the voice told me I was wasting my time, that I needed to have worked on staff at a magazine to have a chance of making it as a freelancer. I needed contacts. I wasn't good enough – the usual. Then once I did send the pitches, the voice told me the editors would be sitting in their plush offices laughing their heads off, perhaps calling other staff members in to show them the ridiculous pitch they'd just received from someone deluded enough to think she could write for magazines.

Then I got a commission by email and actually phoned and spoke to the editor. I was thrilled. But my Inner Pessimist (encouraged by my sister!) suggested it was a practical joke, even going so far as to say the editor I spoke to was probably the office cleaner having a laugh at my expense. Weirdly, even after the article had been published, and I'd been paid and commissioned again by the same magazine, the idea that it had been a complete fluke lingered.

These days, when that voice kicks in, I can shut it down fairly quickly. I've also written 'It's all made up!' in pink chalk on my office wall to remind me that the voice in my head – the one that tells me I'm an idiot and asks me what makes me think I am a writer – isn't real, it's just a product of my overactive imagination, which, let's face it, is a bonus for a writer!

My Inner Coach is getting stronger all the time. In fact, she might be stronger than my Inner Pessimist, but it's been a long time coming. Now I try to focus on my achievements and each one builds my confidence. I can now think, 'I've got a book deal, so I can't be as rubbish as I think I am.' I used to be afraid to try in case I failed. Now I know that the only failure is in not trying. So I go for it.

Baby step 3:
The golden glow

Listen to your Inner Coach more often and the world will become a different place. It will help you begin to create a way of working, living and being that works for you. Even more important, you will be able to identify what you really, really want. You've probably been listening to your Inner Pessimist for so long that you've lost touch with this.

Most of us had our childhood dreams and aspirations kicked out of us years ago, and as a result, we have no idea what we want to do with our lives. At some point, our teachers, parents or friends have told us to get a grip; that we'd never be an astronaut, but had we thought about accounting? That it was perhaps best that we settled down, got married and had a couple of kids like everyone else and give up any ideas of becoming a ballerina. Most of us at some time or other in our lives were told to 'get real'.

It's no good blaming our parents or teachers, though. They thought they were doing the best for us. They lived in a world ruled by their own Inner Pessimist. 'It's a tough old world out there, and you'll get awfully disappointed with silly dreams like that,' they said. We believed them, learning to override the championing of our Inner Coach and fall into step with a world ruled by our Inner Pessimist.

In this part of the Big Leap process, we're going to dig around and start getting you back in touch with what you love, what you enjoy doing and what makes your heart sing. I call it 'golden glow' living, and it is the way we live when we listen to our Inner Coach. To live in the golden glow, you need to work out what you really want, what makes you happy and what you value most.

Here, you can measure what works for you and what's right for you by checking in with your emotional compass, rather than with a checklist of 'shoulds'. You'll know when you're there because life will feel completely right. You'll be able to make decisions with your hand on your heart, saying, 'Yes, this is right.' Those decisions will be based on what makes you feel good about yourself, not on someone else's rules.

The truth is, most of us grew up living our lives by someone else's rules; playing the roles that society demanded we play in order to be 'happy'. We passed exams, launched ourselves on a career path, and then bought the car and the house to go with them. We did all the 'right' things, lived by all the 'right' rules. Now, though, we can't understand why we're not happy and are so desperately resentful and exhausted.

To live a different kind of life, start living by your own rules and rediscover what you want for yourself. It's time to create your own new rulebook: your very own touchstone for life.

10 signs that you're living a life by someone else's rules

1. It takes you hours to make a decision (because deep down you haven't got a clue about what you really want/what's really important to you).
2. You constantly end up doing things you don't want to do and feel resentful.
3. You always search for an 'expert' to help you – you never trust your own instincts.
4. You appear to 'have it all', but still feel something is missing.
5. You envy enthusiastic and passionate people – what are they so excited about?
6. You feel directionless.
7. You dread going to work every day, but you do it because it pays the bills.
8. You hate going clothes shopping because you don't know what suits you.
9. You find yourself complaining and gossiping about other people because it makes you feel better about your own life.
10. You're surrounded by people who complain and gossip about other people. (You're often worried that if you leave the room, they'll be doing the same about you.)

First, you need to design and build your life on your values. When you do that, you will feel the golden glow and be able to create a life for yourself that feels magical and deeply fulfilling.

Ready to leap

EXERCISE: THE GOLDEN GLOW

Look back over the past week (or longer) and remember 10 golden moments – moments that you loved, that gave you a warm, fuzzy glow. Write your answers in your journal.

Part 1
Identify the fuzzy moment and what you were doing.

Part 2
Write down what you valued in that moment. As an example, here are my top five golden moments.

Golden moment 1:
Waking up and not having to do anything I don't want to do that day.
What do I value? Space and freedom.

Golden moment 2:
Coaching a client and connecting with that person; talking to my friends.
What do I value? Connecting on a deep level with people.

Golden moment 3:
Watching inspiring films and reading inspiring books
What do I value? Inspiration.

Golden moment 4:
Learning how to scuba-dive
What do I value? Learning to master something new.

Golden moment 5:
Brainstorming and coming up with ideas for articles, books and magazines
What do I value? Creating new ideas

My values are:
- Space and freedom
- Connecting with people
- Feeling inspired
- Learning to master new things
- Creating new ideas

Part 3
Now list your values in your journal.

Marc Lockley, Big Leaping from Head of Agency Sales to business owner, author and online columnist

I thought I'd take a few months off before diving into building my coaching business, but three weeks in and I was bored! As I identified my values, I soon realized why. One of my top values is connecting with people – it's what I do naturally; why I was attracted to building a coaching business and why I was good at selling and managing in my job. Left to my own devices, going to the gym, chilling out, creating a business on my own, I missed people. So I got a job as a driver for the Wimbledon tennis season. I also offered to supervise exams at my local school. Instantly, I felt so much happier – I was fulfilling three of my top values – connecting with others, giving back and making a difference.

When I was working a 60-hour week, if someone would have told me that I'd be unhappy just chilling out at home, I wouldn't have believed them. But now I realize it's living your values that fulfils you. Discover what you enjoy, what you do naturally, what gives you that sense of flow, and do it every day. That's the secret.

Needs versus values

When first introduced to the concept of golden glow living, many of my clients get confused between unmet needs (see Big Leap Step 2) and values. What is the difference between a need and a value? Our values are what we are naturally attracted to doing if left to our own devices. We don't need to be motivated to 'get inspired' or 'learn new things' – we just want to. We choose to build a life around our values.

On the other hand, our needs are like urgent emotional cravings. We feel we have no choice but to get them met. We are driven to meet our unmet emotional needs, while our values are based on what we really want.

- Values are the currency with which your Inner Coach rewards you for listening.
- Unmet needs are the fuel for your Inner Pessimist's fear and desperation.

10 ways to recognize a value

1. It's something you look forward to indulging yourself in. You don't need anyone to motivate you to do it.
2. It's something you'll probably have done as a child. For example, if creativity is one of your values, you may have written short stories in your spare time, or if entertaining is one of your values, you may have tap-danced for your aunties.
3. It's something you are naturally interested in – it's the specialist magazine you always buy and look forward to reading.
4. It's a theme that runs through your life. If 'freedom' is one of your values, you might have a freelance career and travel a lot.

5. It's something that makes you feel fulfilled and relaxed, not driven and anxious.
6. It's something that gives you a golden glow moment when you do it.
7. It's something you do sooner rather than later.
8. It's something you're naturally good at.
9. It's something that doesn't involve trying to prove anything to anyone.
10. It's something that makes you feel happy.

So what would you love doing if you had an hour, a day or a few weeks? Do a quick experiment with me before you read on. Write a list of the top 20 things that you love to do. No, really, do it now – be it drinking wine with your best friend or building models out of matchsticks, just write it all down. Once you've written your list you can read on. (But don't cheat!)

Andrew Stone, 32, Big Leaping from journalist on a trade magazine to globetrotting as a travel-guide writer

I just thought I was a bit different. While everyone else wanted to settle down in a steady job, I had this deep-seated fear of living a 'groundhog day' life – every day the same. I always knew I wasn't happy in an office. But it wasn't until I identified my values and needs that I understood why.

My top two values in life are adventure and fun. I have a need for freedom, but not for security. That's why I am happiest travelling in a tiny town in Madagascar with £2.50 in my pocket – enough for bus fare and breakfast – travelling on a wing and a prayer. Once you've identified your values and needs, you can then set goals that will actually make you happy rather than goals that you think you should set to please other people.

Find your flow

So far, we have a list of what you do to enjoy yourself. Now let's discover if these things will make you happy.

In the last few years, there has been an explosion of research into the scientifically based idea of 'positive psychology'. Making an interesting distinction between pleasure and gratification, Martin Seligman, founder of the positive psychology movement and author of over 20 books, such as *Learned Optimism and What You Can Change and What You Can't,* suggests that our pursuit of 'easy pleasure' over gratification might hinder our feelings of fulfilment:

> *It is very puzzling that we often choose pleasure (and worse, displeasure) over gratification. In the nightly choice between reading a good book and watching a sitcom on television, we often choose the latter – although surveys show again and again that the average mood while watching sitcoms on television is mild depression.*

Seligman theorizes that the depression epidemic could be due to an over-reliance on shortcuts to happiness, be it shopping or chocolate. 'What would happen if my entire life were made up of such easy pleasures, never calling on my strengths, never presenting challenges? Such a life sets one up for depression,' he says.

Seligman is not saying that pleasure does not have its place, but that when we chase only pleasure we can feel empty. Our brain chemistry doesn't help. Pleasure-seeking involves two ancient regions of the brain, the amygdala and the nucleus accumbens, which communicate using the chemical dopamine to form the brain's reward system. Pleasure-seeking triggers the production of dopamine, which keeps you coming back for more – it's insatiable. So you are forever left wanting.

Exercise: DISTINGUISHING PLEASURE FROM GRATIFICATION

Ready **?** to leap

Write down the answers to the following in your Big Leap journal.

Part 1

Working from your list of the top 20 things that you love to do, ask yourself:

- Which ones give you that quick-fix 'pleasurable' buzz?
- What makes you feel good instantly, but leaves you wanting more?

Part 2

Now ask yourself:

- What role does pleasure play in your life?
- Is it something that enhances your life and makes you feel alive or is it a compensation for being somewhat at odds with your life?
- Are you desperately reaching out for fun, fun, fun: drinking too much, over-shopping, anything to numb your feelings and make you feel better about your life?
- What positive and negative effects does your pleasure-seeking have on your life?
- Do you motivate yourself with a reward system? For example, treat yourself to a glass of wine at the end of the day for a day well lived? But does the glass spill over to half a bottle or a bottle?
- What effect does that have on your energy levels and health? If shopping is your greatest source of pleasure and you reward yourself after a week at work with a shopping spree – are you in debt?

A satisfied life

Living a life based on your values usually means you are living in the 'flow' of life. This is not some hippy philosophy, but one based on 30 years of research by Mihaly Csikszentmihalyi, Professor of Psychology and Management at Claremont Graduate College, California, who studied thousands of people to discover what makes our lives meaningful and satisfying. From his research, he wrote a book called *Flow: The Psychology of Optimal Experience*. 'Flow' is what he describes as being involved in an activity that narrows our attention, giving us a sense of being absorbed and a feeling of transcendence.

The great news is that any activity can lead to flow: playing a game, listening to music, writing a novel, etc. In spite of the huge differences in the activities themselves, those who've experienced it – from meditating Buddhists to motorcycle gang members, chess players to assembly line workers – describe the psychological components of flow in notably similar ways:

- It happens when you're focusing on a challenging task that requires skill.
- The task requires concentration.
- There are clear goals.
- You get immediate feedback.
- Your involvement is deep and effortless.
- There is a sense of control.
- Your sense of self vanishes.
- Time stops.

Exercise: FIND YOUR FLOW

Ready
to leap

Answer the following in your journal:

- What do you love doing that always gives you a feeling of satisfaction afterwards?
- What activity engrosses you so much that when you look up, five hours has gone by?
- What do you love to focus on?
- What do you always long to get back to?

Courage to just do it

When you first start working out what you really want, it can feel as if you are being selfish. What if what you want doesn't fit with what your family wants? Many of us are simply not used to living a life based on what we truly want.

In fact, by acting selfish, we find we are much happier, generally much nicer people, and are able to give from a truly loving place. But, like anything else, your 'I'll do what I want' muscles will be flabby after years of little use.

Exercise: JUST SAY NO

Ready
to leap

Buy yourself some time and space to do what you truly want by saying 'no'.

Say 'no' 10 times in the next seven days to anything that sounds remotely uninteresting. Every time you say 'no' to something you don't want to do, you're creating space to say 'yes' to what you really, really want to do.

Baby step 4:
The bingo moment

You've left the void of fear, you've had a wild old time in la-la land, you're getting clear about what gives you that golden glow – so now what? I'm hoping that you'll get the 'bingo moment' soon, and I suggest you do nothing until you do. The bingo moment literally hits you between the eyes. When it happens, you'll think, 'That's it! This is the kind of life I want to create.' You'll feel alive, excited and so revved up that you'll want to dance up and down on the spot with glee. The bingo moment is when you find a career or lifestyle or community that is orientated around your values.

I used to be a journalist and knew it wasn't making me happy, but I didn't have a clue what I wanted to do next. I had always wanted to be a writer – I thought that was my dream – so when I retrained to become a writer and found out that it wasn't what I really wanted, I was stuck. I hired a coach, but no matter how hard I looked to find a new path, nothing inspired me.

Then, the week before Christmas, I was interviewing an expert for an article on how to survive the festive season and thought, 'Oh no, this is the same tired old advice. I could do better than this.' Then bingo! Yes! I could do better than this. I could train to be a coach. Even though I had been working with a coach, it had never occurred to me that I could become one. In that moment, I knew that was what I wanted to do. It was like a lightning flash.

The next day, I enrolled on a course and stumped up the cash for coach training.

Looking back, I can see that all roads led me to coaching: the voluntary work I'd done as a mentor and that I had enjoyed so much, my interest in self-development that had led me as a journalist to interview some of the biggest gurus of our time, my fascination with personal development. Not least, I had hired a coach long before it had been popularized in the UK and I was deeply impressed by the results I had achieved. I had the evidence for myself that coaching worked, as it had improved my life in a very sustainable and dramatic way.

So here was something I completely believed in and was completely orientated around four of my top five values: connecting with people, freedom (I could run my own business and work from home), inspiration and learning. Now, I'm writing about it, so am fulfilling my fifth value of creating new ideas. Bingo!

All these thoughts came afterwards, but my 'bingo moment' was when I just knew what the next step was for me. It's a powerful feeling, and for you to make the Big Leap, it's important that you feel it, too.

10 signs that you're having a bingo moment

1. You feel sick with excitement.
2. You ring all your friends and say, 'You'll never guess what I'm going to be/do!'
3. You scream 'Eureka!' in the bath.
4. You wake up very excited, with a smile on your face, and go straight to the computer and start researching.
5. You don't do any work at the office because you're too busy surfing the Internet for information.
6. You start ringing colleges, training organizations or estate agents to find out what needs to be done to make the leap.

7. You start noticing other people on the train reading articles or seeing programmes on TV that all confirm you're doing the right thing.
8. You ring up your best friend a dozen times a day because you want to talk to someone endlessly about this.
9. You feel impatient and raring to go – your sights are fixed firmly on the future.
10. You become very critical of the life you have now.

Marc Lockley, Big Leaping from Head of Agency Sales to business owner, author and online columnist

My bingo moment about writing a book came when I was buying a car. I was sitting in a car salesroom and there was a woman next to me buying exactly the same car – except she paid £4,000 more for it.

I thought it was outrageous. I had taken my negotiation skills for granted, but realized in that moment that perhaps I had some valuable skills to teach. I pitched the book idea How to Pay Less for More *to a publisher the very next week. It was published in 2008.*

Let's do some digging

We sometimes have to dig around in our past to find some clues before we get our bingo moment. Don't dismiss anything or get trapped in practicalities.

Many of us see a glimmer: 'Well, I quite liked story-writing as a child,' but dismiss it quickly. 'I can't change profession to be a writer at this stage!' We don't give ourselves permission to explore the idea thoroughly. Try this exercise to see if any themes or patterns begin to emerge.

Exercise: PREPARING THE GROUND FOR YOUR BINGO MOMENT

Ready to leap **?**

Answer the following questions in your journal as truthfully and fully as possible, without editing yourself.

- What was your childhood dream before you came to believe that what you wanted to do was unrealistic and told yourself to take your head out of the clouds?
- Who have you viciously envied recently and why? Envy is a great tool for telling us what we really want. What have they got that you want?
- What are you naturally good at – what do you do effortlessly?
- What do you love doing – when you do this time seems to slip away?
- Who do you love spending time with?
- What have seen on television or read about in a magazine or newspaper that stirred your interest?
- What are you passionate about?
- What did you love doing as a child?
- If you didn't have to prove that you were good enough, what would you do with the rest of your life?

Still stuck?

You can't force your bingo moment. If you get to the end of this chapter and haven't developed a clear vision of the life that awaits you, don't panic. There isn't a specific route to get there. You can't fill in questionnaire A, form B and personality test C and get your bingo. It's more organic than that. However, the key thing is that you must be willing. If you are open to what your next step is, you'll start to receive some answers. You simply have to ask.

Ready to leap

Exercise: LISTENING TO THE WHISPERS

1. **What question do you want to pose?**
   What are you trying to find the answer to? Think carefully. You can make the question specific, e.g. what is the next step during the next three months? Or you can make the question big, e.g. what is the purpose of my life? Whatever your question, write it down and then place it in one or two (or ten) places where you'll see it every day.

2. **Be willing to hear the answer**
   The answer may come when you see something that inspires you, or when a friend starts talking about something that makes you feel a rush of excitement, or when someone rings up and offers you a job.

3. **Feel it, know it**
   There is no ambiguity about the bingo moment. You feel it and it feels right. There's no 'Ooh, I'm not sure,' about it. Your Inner Coach usually tells you straight. If you're still humming and hawing, then keep asking questions to try to get clarity. Have patience: sometimes it doesn't happen overnight (although sometimes it does).

4. **Follow the whispers**
   The answers don't always come in one big, booming bingo moment. Remember that your Inner Coach talks in whispers through your feelings and body. Start noticing any kind of clues about how you're feeling, such as excitement, a skip of joy, any slight rush of emotion. Look at the feeling, focus on it and ask, 'What is exciting me here? What is it about this situation that makes me happy?' If you don't get an answer immediately, you will, just keep asking.

Exercise: WHAT ARE YOU TRYING TO PROVE?

Ready
to leap **?**

Creating a new way of living, working or being means focusing on enjoyment, fulfilment and inspiration. It means letting go of fear, struggle and having to 'motivate yourself'. You no longer have to prove anything to anyone. You are simply getting on with doing what you love.

You will feel intuitively that you are on the right path. Your gut instinct will be screaming, 'yes, yes, yes!' When you pause to think, you may not be sure this is the answer but. for once, your Inner Pessimist is being outshone by your Inner Coach doing somersaults in your stomach. It is a very strong sense – which you may not be able to justify logically – that you're heading in the right direction.

One great way of testing whether your bingo moment truly leads to the right path for you (and whether you are motivated by your unmet needs or your values) is to ask yourself these questions:

- Could I spend the next five years living this way because I genuinely love it?
- When I visualize this life in great detail, does it make me feel good?
- If I had nothing to prove to anyone, would I spend my time following this path?
- Do I feel confident that I know how to take the next three steps to making this happen?
- Do I feel excited rather than drained?
- Does my heart leap rather than sink?
- Do I want to start right now?

Baby step 5:
Create the vision

Once you've had your bingo moment, it's time to get serious with your la-la land vision. The next step is to start to make that vision a reality.

Ready to leap

Exercise: A LIFE IN THE DAY

The la-la land journalist has now gone home, but she's asked if she can come back tomorrow with a film crew to document your ideal day. In your journal, describe what the viewer will see in your life-in-a-day documentary.

- Where do you wake up?
- How do you wake up?
- What's the first thing you do when you wake?
- Describe the people who are sharing your life.
- How do you behave around each other?
- What are you wearing? How do you look?
- How do you spend your morning?
- What do you do for lunch? Where do you go?
- How do you spend your afternoon?
- Describe how you end your day.
- How do you spend your evening? With whom?
- What is the highlight of the programme?
- What message are you consistently giving out to the people around you?
- What impression is the viewer left with?
- What do people say to their friends about the documentary when they are discussing it the next day?

Nicky Hambleton-Jones, Big Leaping from management consultant to celebrity fashion stylist

Think big when you write your vision. You don't have to know how you're going to get there. I always knew I wanted my own TV series and I wrote that in my vision, but I had no idea how that was going to happen. I had absolutely no contacts in television. I was just a nobody with a new business. But in the end, the TV production company came to me.

So when you write your vision, be bold. Don't worry about the 'how', just focus on what you really want to create for yourself.

Getting 'there'

This 'creating the vision' exercise comes with a warning. When we have a big vision, there is a danger of living for the future and not in the present. We say to ourselves, 'When I get "there", I'll be happy.' We say, 'When I'm thin/famous/doing my dream job/married to my dream partner/living in Sydney/in my house in the country [you fill in the blanks], then I'll finally be happy.'

We learn this story from childhood fairytales. We watch knights fight the dragon, princesses marry the prince, heroes slay the beast, struggling through their journey to get 'there', and then all living happily ever after.

But I don't want you to wait until the end of the story to be happy. I want you to be happy now.

This book is not about swapping one kind of struggle for another. Why go to all this trouble to remove the grind of commuting and a life that exhausts you, simply to set yourself up to struggle even more to build your ideal life, just waiting for the day you can finally get there? If we have been attending to our unmet needs and are building a life around our values and what we love to do, we can put this vision away. We don't have to struggle to create it, we don't have to set goals or motivate ourselves. We will simply be doing what we love to do.

Once we've identified what we want, our vision magically starts to fall into place. This explains why so many of my Big Leap clients achieve so much, so quickly.

The amount of struggle you encounter on your Big Leap journey is in direct proportion to the amount of time you spend listening to your Inner Pessimist, and whether or not you are attending to your unmet needs. (The more unmet needs you have, the louder your Inner Pessimist tends to scream.)

The Big Leap journey can be a rich and satisfying one if you find your bingo moment, discover how to listen to your Inner Coach and live a golden glow existence. We don't have to wait until we get 'there' to experience what we want. We're there already.

Don't put your happiness on hold

In my la-la land, I've written an Oscar-winning screenplay, won the Man Booker Prize and created an Oprah-style web portal in the UK that inspires people every day. What kind of life do you live in your la-la land?

The next question I want to ask you is, if you were living it large in la-la land, with all the things, people and maybe that beautiful yacht that you think would make you happy – how are you hoping it might make you feel? Free? Loved? Secure? Respected?

The Big Leap in thinking is realizing that the yacht won't make you feel free, it will just take you from A to B and will probably be great fun to sail. However, you can have freedom in your life right now by changing the way you think. Freedom, peace, love – they are internal states.

I know it's a leap. I know I would be so happy if I won that Oscar! But for how long? I thought I'd be happy when I became a journalist, when I became Health Editor of a national magazine, when I became a successful coach, when I became a mother, when I moved to the country – and I was and am. But then I'm scanning the horizon for more. Back on that treadmill, running faster and faster, and going nowhere.

Many of us may think winning prizes or earning more money will make us happy. This is simply not true. Nobel Prize-winning researcher Dr Daniel Kahneman found that it is a complete myth that wealth brings happiness. On researching people's reported happiness and life satisfaction, he found that people are likely to overrate the joy-bringing effect of whatever they're thinking about at the time, whether it's money or the number of dates they had last week.

What he discovered is that an increase in income actually has a relatively brief effect on life satisfaction; that when countries experience a sudden rise in wealth, there is not a corresponding increase in citizens' sense of well-being. Life satisfaction does tend to increase as a nation's per capita income rises, but there is little increase in life satisfaction once it goes above $12,000 a year.

Finally, studies show that the wealthier people are, the more intense the negative emotions they experience. None of these studies link wealth to a greater experience of happiness. So be careful what you wish for! Things, money and a fancy lifestyle will not make us feel peaceful or happy in the long run. We long for them because we think they will make us feel differently.

Ready to leap

> **Exercise: VISUALIZING HAPPINESS**
>
> Think of a time when you felt completely happy. Where are you? Who are you with? What are you doing? What can you see? What can you hear? What can you smell? You're feeling content, happy, fulfilled – where are you feeling it in your body? Let that feeling expand up, down and sideways. Let it flow out the top of your head and through your feet. How does it feel?
>
> There. Happiness by simply closing your eyes. Who needs an Oscar?

Baby step 6:
Setting goals in the present

In warning against 'if only' thinking, I'm not saying we can't set goals. Just be careful about 'I'll be happy when …' goals. My la-la land vision is based on my values – creativity, inspiration, connecting with others. Yes, it would be lovely to win an Oscar, but in the meantime I can still enjoy living my values by setting goals that make me happy every day, goals that I will enjoy engaging with on a daily basis.

The important distinction to make is to take pleasure in the journey rather than it being all about the destination. This gives you permission to start small, allowing you to enjoy yourself more thoroughly. For example, learning to run a 5-kilometre race, and then working up to a local 10-kilometre fun run, congratulating yourself on each step, rather than waiting until you've run the marathon before you can feel like you've achieved something.

Exercise: ENJOYING THE JOURNEY

Ready to leap

Answer the following in your journal.

- What goals can you set that are about enjoying the present?
- How can you express your values right here, right now?
- If your la-la land is about climbing Mt Everest, ask yourself why. What would that achievement give you? Adventure? Freedom? What goals can you set that would allow you to be adventurous and free on a daily basis?

Your Inner Pessimist is probably saying right now ...

'What a crock. I am so bored of this. You know this is complete crap, don't you? How are you going to survive living a "golden glow life" – whatever that means? What about the money, honey? You're going to give up your well-paid job and do what? Become a flower-wearing fairy dancer earning a pittance an hour? I don't think so! It really is just la-la land. You can never do this in a month of Sundays. You know that, don't you? For God's sake, don't waste any more time or energy thinking about stuff like this, you're just going to make a massive fool of yourself. These Big Leapers, they're different – they've probably all got a trust fund to fall back on, or they're just brainier and more talented than you. I admire you for thinking about all this, but let's get real, shall we? Have you actually read your vision? C'mon, enough with the joking around. Good try, but I think it's time you stopped fooling yourself. This "Big Leap" process is never going to work for you, you're simply not brave, talented or clever enough.'

What you need to be doing right now ...

Tune in to your Inner Coach. Write down in your journal what she has to say in response.

The Big Belief

'We're off to see the Wizard, the Wonderful Wizard of Oz.'

*'We are what we think.
All that we are arises
with our thoughts.
With our thoughts,
We make our world.'*

– BUDDHA
(*c*.563–*c*. 483 BCE)

Big Leap Step 4:   **THE BABY STEPS**

1. What colour is your filter?
2. What is the cost of your self-beliefs?
3. New belief – new world
4. 'I am a sex god': acting 'as if'
5. Cultivating awareness

If you really want to change your life, you need to change the way you think, the decisions you make, and, most importantly, what you believe. What we believe about ourselves and our life is our reality. In this step of the Big Leap journey, you need to identify what you believe now, which is creating your present reality, and then look at what you'd have to believe to create a reality that you adore. Your mind won't change overnight, but if you decide to take a different stance on some old beliefs that have stopped you from moving forward in the past, then you will find that life feels very different. Like Dorothy in *The Wizard of Oz*, the goal of this step is to begin to realize that there is no wizard out there who is going to save you; you have everything you need to save yourself.

What you're probably thinking at Big Leap Step 4

- I can't do this!
- I've had a slight flight of fancy, but now it's time to get back to reality.
- Who am I to think I could ever create this vision?
- When have I got the time to even think about achieving this?
- Imagine if this were possible? But it's not, so I better forget it.

What you're probably doing at Big Leap Step 4

- Telling someone about your plans, seeing the look on their face and feeling incredibly foolish.
- Stammering when you say what you want to do
- Telling people about the kind of life you'd like to create for yourself and then laughing uproariously as if you were joking.
- Stomping around feeling angry, saying, 'What the hell do I think I'm doing?'
- Isolating yourself, not talking to anyone about how you're feeling, especially loved ones.
- Feeling emotional, alone and crazy.

Brace yourself. This is the part of the process when you actually get to make the Big Leap. Although if you are still under the impression that making the leap is about changing the externals of your life, you may need to think again. Yes, material things do change along the way, but the real change is in what and how you think. A radical shift in thinking involves changing assumptions we have made about our life.

So the good news, or the bad news, however you want to
see it, is that it's all in your head. Our thoughts and beliefs
define our world. If you believe the world is a harsh and
cruel place, that's how it will feel. But if you choose to
believe that anything is possible, that life will come to
meet you halfway, and that your efforts will be rewarded,
then that is what you'll experience.

What do you believe about yourself? What do you believe
about life? Do you believe that it is wonderful and easy,
that things will always work out, that you are priceless,
that you deserve only the best? Do you believe you will
always be supported, that you'll always land on your feet?
Do you believe that life is fun, and that you always attract
the best there is to offer?

Or do you believe that life is hard, money is the root of
evil, all men are bastards, all women are fickle, survival is
a struggle, men don't commit, women cheat, and the rich
are lonely and cold-hearted? Do you believe you'll never
make it because you're not good enough, that you're
worthless, oh, and stupid, too?

What is your reality? What do you believe to be true
about yourself and the wider world? Because whatever
you believe, you're right. The woman who believes that
all men cheat and life is a bitch and then you die is right.
The man who believes that all women are angels and life
is one long party is right, too. They're right because they
believe this to be true. Make the leap, change your beliefs,
and you can change your reality.

If you don't believe me, ask the scientists. Quantum
physics has taught us that our world is what we perceive
it to be. Reality is simply raw, unformed data waiting to
be interpreted by you, the perceiver. We take a 'radically
ambiguous, flowing quantum soup' as the physicists call

it, and use our perception to make sense of it. But our perception can be radically different from the next person's perception. Take this thinking to its ultimate conclusion, and you can change your world, your body and your life by simply changing your beliefs. Isn't that an exciting and liberating thought?

Lynne McNicoll, Big Leaping from housewife to running her own business and becoming a charity fundraiser

My old belief was, 'I'm not good enough.' I was surprised when I recognized that my belief went back all the way to my childhood. Actually not just surprised, I was sad. How many years had I let slip by without grabbing opportunities? How much had this belief cost me?

Changing this belief has been a gradual process. With my coach, I agreed that I had to change my focus – from only seeing evidence to support the view that I wasn't good enough to creating evidence to prove that I am.

It was a process of baby steps and big leaps. Baby steps included my very supportive partner writing out a dozen stickers with the word 'confident' on them and putting them on kitchen cupboards, doors, the tomato sauce bottle (!) and mirrors.

My Big Leap was starting my own 'Virtual Assistant' business. A virtual assistant is like a PA, but works for several clients at home. I wanted to go back to work again, but I didn't want to go back to working nine to five. My coach helped me identify what I was good at – organization, administration and looking after people – and I realized that I could create the perfect working environment at home. It was also the perfect 'belief-building' environment. I would be doing things day in, day out that I knew I could do well, building my new belief that I was good enough. Not that I don't wobble sometimes. The best fear-

buster I've discovered is to write down any problem and break it into manageable pieces. This works for anything from phone calls to fitness schedules. Baby steps are the best way to create change. When I was terrified of phoning clients, I wrote down step by step what I was going to say because when I'm scared my mind freezes. Every time I take a baby step, it is another piece of evidence that I use to prove to myself, and the world, that I am good enough. My confidence grows daily. You can take a baby step, and then another, and a year later you can see the difference – and it's phenomenal.

Baby step 1:
What colour is your filter?

I think that beliefs are like filters: we fit them just behind our eyes and look through them at life. We are not born with our filters, rather we create them (albeit unconsciously) one at a time. As we go through life, we slot them into place. We usually start with our parents' beliefs, and then move on to our friends' beliefs, and then the beliefs of our teachers, our peers, our employers, our society and our culture. By about the age of 21 (although some say the process is complete by the time we are 10 years old), we have our filters well and truly in place. These filters help us make assumptions about how life is, how life will treat us, how to behave and not behave. They are usually totally unconscious; we simply assume that how we see the world is the way the world actually is.

When I first got my head around this, I felt my mind begin to melt. I realized that my beliefs are not the truth; they are not the way things really are. In fact, I had to face the fact that there might not be a reality the way I'd always understood it to be. 'You mean that I just made it all up?' I asked my coach. 'Well, yes,' she said. 'Beliefs are simply opinions that stay in place because we never question them. They become part of our subconscious and form the cornerstones of the reality that we experience – our worlds. We then validate our beliefs by selecting evidence that will support them, editing out anything else (if we even see it) that disagrees or challenges our belief system, because it's too threatening.' That's why it usually requires a dramatic piece of evidence to 'shake' our beliefs.

Petra, a Big Leap client, lived her life with a very old filter in place – one that was 30 years old. She believed she was stupid. 'But you're a television producer,' I protested. 'I've had to work so hard to get here and to stay here, you have no idea,' she would say, scurrying off to work yet another weekend.

When Petra was six, she was kept down a year at school. 'From that moment on, I knew that I was the stupid one. It was so humiliating.' Petra had originally come to coaching because she didn't feel she had a life outside her job. She soon discovered her real problem was that she spent inordinate amounts of energy trying to prove to everyone she wasn't as 'thick' as she thought she was. A little game she'd set up ever since she left school and got a first-class honours degree at Bristol University!

She worked very hard, but even when she got the accolades – the job positions that proved she was anything but stupid – she was terrified someone would find her out and discover her success was in some way a fluke. Petra had plenty of evidence to the contrary, but because she believed she was stupid, she refused to see it – until she started to look at beliefs and how they are formed. Then she could see how she had locked herself into her very own self-made prison. She could literally pinpoint the moment when she formed this belief – it was when she experienced the horror and shame she felt at being held back at school. Once she had decided that she was stupid, nothing could shift this belief. It formed and dried as hard as concrete at the age of six. Now, at the age of 36, she was still lugging this lump of concrete around with her wherever she went.

It can be quite horrifying when we start to look at our beliefs and filters and realize how they have affected our lives. In fact, it would really be easier to ignore this step. Maybe you're thinking, 'Looking at my beliefs? I don't need to do that,' before you quietly turn the page. But that's just fear talking. If you change your beliefs, you're going to move out of your comfort zone – quite dramatically – and your Inner Pessimist will do anything to stop you doing that. So if you find that your Inner Pessimist is shouting loudly at this point, just smile, wave and be brave. Courage is needed for this next step.

Our old beliefs keep us safely in our comfort zone. If you believe that life is hard, that men don't commit, that women are unfaithful, that no one really finds their dream career or that you're not good enough, talented enough or beautiful enough to create the life that you really want, you can avoid having to risk living to your full potential. You know that to do so, you would have to start taking risks: which might mean failure, being wrong and, possibly, loss.

Most of us are only willing to do this when life doesn't seem to be working as well as we think it should. If you're suffering, it's a good indication that you may have some limiting self-beliefs in place. We just have to figure out what they are.

Exercise: WHAT DO YOU BELIEVE ABOUT YOURSELF?

Ready to leap ?

Answer the following in your journal.

- What decision would a child need to have made to survive in your family?
- What happens to people like you?
- What will people say about you when you're dead?
- What negative feeling do you experience most often?
- When you get this feeling, what do you believe about yourself?
- When you get this feeling, what do you believe about life?
- What would you have to believe about yourself to have a career like yours?
- What would you have to believe about yourself to have a relationship history like yours?
- What would you have to believe about yourself to have a circle of friends like yours?
- What would you have to believe about yourself, or life, for things to be exactly how they are right now?

Nicky Hambleton-Jones, Big Leaping from management consultant to celebrity fashion stylist

I had loads of negative beliefs kicking around. The main one was that I would never make it, that I was a 'loser'. I'd gone from job to job and I couldn't make it work, so why on earth did I think my business idea would?

I wrote all my negative beliefs on a piece of paper and realized how much unconscious energy I actually gave them. When I wrote them down, they did seem faintly ridiculous. So I created a new mantra, 'I am happy to succeed, I am happy to fail, but I choose success.' I was embracing the possibility of failing, because sometimes I was stressing myself out by running away from the idea of failure. But when I actually surrendered to the thought that it could happen, it took all the sting away.

Baby step 2:
What is the cost of your self-beliefs?

Petra was horrified when she identified the real reason she didn't have a social life: that she believed she was stupid and spent all of her time overcompensating to try to prove the contrary.

As you will discover in this step, it is possible to create a whole personality as a means of compensating for our negative self-beliefs. When we don't believe we're good enough inside, we will try all sorts of ways to disguise it on the outside, but it will always feel like a hollow victory. Our cars, our clothes and our careers scream 'fake, fake, fake', because deep down, we feel we are pretending. The fear of discovery follows us wherever we go. We fear that if we didn't have our protective layer of possessions, careers and appearance, we would be exposed.

It isn't uncommon for many of us to spend our whole lives running away from that fear of being uncovered as the useless loser or dunce that we believe we are deep-down. No matter how we dress it up – in Jimmy Choo shoes or a high-flying career – we can't hide from ourselves the feeling of worthlessness we have inside. For many, fear is a great motivator – and the greater the fear, the greater the motivation to be successful. Through coaching my clients, I have discovered that sometimes the most successful people are the most terrified.

What is the price of success on this basis? If success is simply compensation for negative beliefs, anyone who lives in fear can never rest or be still – they must always achieve. They will always want to get 'there' – to be thin, to be rich, to be happy – because they think that when they reach this place, they will be able to rest and the fear will go away. What they don't realize is that the fear will never go away until they address what they truly believe about themselves.

Petra's self-belief had served her well in that she had been very successful in her career. Her fear of being found out had made her push herself to grand heights. But with a negative belief system like Petra's, she was always driven, always on the go, because she could never be or have enough – because she could never feel that 'herself' was enough.

So, like Petra, it may seem as if your negative belief system has been serving you well on some level, but in the end, if you don't face it, it will cost you more. This is why our self-beliefs are so tough to admit and to come to terms with. When you look at what a belief has cost you in your life, it can add up to frightening proportions emotionally, as well as financially.

Petra realized her belief was costing her – big time. She was so busy trying to prove she wasn't stupid that she didn't have time to create a relationship. She was worried that time was running out and she wouldn't be able to have a baby. Her health was also suffering, as stress was aggravating her eczema. 'I'm a mess!' she wailed. 'And I'm stupid.' 'You are if you believe you are,' I said. 'Not helpful,' she snapped.

Lynne McNicoll, Big Leaping from housewife to running her own business and becoming a charity fundraiser

My old beliefs have cost me dearly. By the time I sought coaching, I had left a good job some years ago. I was emotionally drained. I was simply unable to cope. I was also very overweight. I felt like a doormat with my family: 'Lynne'll do it.'

I rarely refused, because I thought it might buy me some brownie points. Funny that, it never did. In fact, I felt like I got even less respect. Even my partner, who had never wavered and had always given me full and unswerving support, could not convince me I was a really worthy person capable of much, much more. My new beliefs have transformed my life. I have a life I love. I know change can and does happen. It has happened to me.

I feel I am now coming out of a shell that I had been building for years. I've met several new friends and the diversity they bring to my life is significant and welcome. I am seeing more of old friends who I had neglected (I thought there was little point in seeing them as they wouldn't be interested in me – would they?). Where it is appropriate, I can say 'No' to my family, and they don't seem to have suffered as a result. I now believe that I am more confident, enabled and empowered. I can do it!

Ready to leap

Exercise: ADDING UP THE COSTS

List your negative self-beliefs in your journal. For each belief, write the answers to the questions below

- What is this belief costing you emotionally?
- What is this belief costing you financially?
- What is this belief costing you in your relationships?
- What is this belief costing your health and well-being?

Baby step 3:
New belief – new world

At the beginning, this process requires a massive leap of faith. How can you change a fundamental belief about yourself when it is so ingrained? 'How can I start believing I'm intelligent when, ever since I was six, I've believed I was thick?' asked Petra. Good question.

Once you've identified an old, limiting self-belief, you need to replace it with a new belief, one that serves you better. The way to do this is to decide on your new belief, and then find evidence to support it. After all, what you focus on expands. I discovered that it isn't enough to chant a new belief at myself in the mirror every morning. Affirmations are great, but to really make a new belief strong, it's important to start collecting evidence to really prove to yourself that it's true.

At first, it feels like you're trying to pat your head and rub your stomach at the same time. Having changed the belief, even if you catch yourself in the middle of an old pattern of thinking, 'I'm not clever enough,' you can now notice it and decide to change it to 'I am clever enough.' Then you can support it with, 'I have a degree from Bristol University/I've just been given a promotion/I've just won a Bafta …': whatever makes it true for you.

It can be helpful to look at past evidence to start changing your beliefs, but what I've found to be most useful is to collect evidence every day and write it in a journal. Each day, write five or even ten specific examples of why this new belief is true for you today. As you build evidence, your filter and your focus begin to change. Experiment and play with this idea.

Ready
to leap **?**

Exercise: CREATING NEW BELIEFS

Read each of these statements, and think about how believing it would change your life.

Write in your journal how each belief would change how you approach work, your relationships and your health.

- I am supported and guided in everything I do.
- My potential is limitless.
- I'm not perfect, but I'm lovely/great/wonderful.
- Everyone is doing the best they can.
- This too shall pass.
- The present is exactly as it's supposed to be.
- I embrace change.
- I can learn from every situation.
- I'm okay just the way I am.
- I'm an attractive human being.

Tracy L'Epine, Big Leaping from single and childless to finding the love of her life and having a baby at 40

The media always tends to give women a hard time about leaving motherhood too late. For many of us, it's simply that we haven't met the right person. I was married and divorced in my twenties, so I wasn't automatically looking for a life partner straight away in my thirties.

I always knew I wanted babies. I was a stuntwoman and knew the profession didn't mix well with motherhood, so had retrained at 35 to become a psychotherapist. I was 40 and I thought I'd missed the boat when I met Guy in a bar. It was love at first sight. Within six months I was pregnant. I can't tell you how delighted I was. So I was devastated when I miscarried at eight weeks. I was in utter despair. Not helped by my doctor, who told me that my age was against me. I was in a terrible state. I knew I had to find some help, so I researched on the Internet and found a hypnotherapist who specialized in fertility.

I walked into her office a wreck and came out calm, hopeful and relaxed. I just knew I could get pregnant again. The hypnotherapy got through to my subconscious mind and told it that it was possible to be pregnant. My hypnotherapist explained to me that the mind cannot tell the difference between things that are real and imagined. Two weeks later, I was pregnant. I felt like it was a miracle, but I know now that it's the power of the mind. When you change your beliefs, you change your life – and can even make a new life!

Baby step 4:
'I am a sex god': acting 'as if'

Beliefs don't change overnight, so don't expect it to be an instant process. You have to be committed and persistent. But I believe it is one of the most life-changing processes you can ever commit to. Change a fundamental belief about yourself and you can change your world.

Our beliefs about life and about ourselves form and then come true for us when we find proof to support them. By acting 'as if', we start creating evidence to prove a new belief about ourselves is right. If you believe you've got no talent and you're going to fail, that's exactly what you'll create. But if you believe that you are good enough, the momentum starts to build and your reality begins to change from the inside out. Play with this idea and have some fun.

Ready to leap

Exercise: ACT 'AS IF'

By acting 'as if', you can quickly and rather dramatically adopt a new belief. Choose one of the below and act 'as if' for the next seven days.

What would you do differently for the next seven days ...
- if you believed that you were the sexiest being alive?
- if you believed you had the potential to create a business empire?
- if you believed you were a creative genius?
- if you knew you would always have enough money?
- if you believed you were the most precious being on earth – more precious than your children, husband, best friend, parents?
- if you believed you only had a week to live?
- if you believed your parents loved you?
- if you believed you had a perfect body?
- if you believed you were going to be given everything you ever wanted in the next year?

Baby step 5:
Cultivating awareness

So it's as simple as that then, is it? You identify your self-limiting beliefs, look at what they are costing you, feel miserable for a while, replace them with fabulous new beliefs, and then act 'as if' and you're sorted. Well, kind of. I don't want to spread malicious rumours, but sometimes it's not quite as cut-and-dried as all that.

Even after identifying my 'not good enough' belief and replacing it with a new, shiny 'I am good enough' belief, then amassing lots and lots of evidence to prove it, I still sometimes feel terrible, useless and very below average. I have made my leap, but I still fall flat on my face sometimes. Something or someone will trigger my old way of thinking, and I go straight back into the old 'I'm useless, I'm going to fail, everyone is going to laugh at me,' script. The Inner Pessimist can be just as vicious these days as he could in the early stages.

The difference now, though, is that I catch it sooner. The old fear doesn't get branded into my nerves as much as it used to, and I don't wrestle for days with that old miserable feeling. It may be just a few hours, even minutes, before I realize that it's just my 'not good enough' stuff rattling my cage. In the moment when I observe it in its cage, rather than be in the cage with it, magic happens. In that moment, I can choose to hear another voice; I can choose to think differently. I can choose to make a leap.

I was comforted to hear Richard Alpert (a.k.a. spiritual guru Ram Dass) and author of *Be Here Now* state that in 30 years of intense spiritual work, he has not let go of one of his neuroses. He is simply more aware of them. He can welcome them in: 'Well, hello, paranoia, I haven't seen you for a long time, come on in.' He is no longer paralyzed by his beliefs, and he no longer gets engaged in emotional tussles with his neurotic thoughts. He is detached, watching them like interesting animals at the zoo.

The renowned meditation teacher and writer Stephen Levine talks about seeing thoughts as boxcars on a freight train during meditation. He asks us to imagine standing at a railway crossing, watching a freight train passing by, challenging us to try to keep looking ahead into the present, rather than being pulled towards looking into each of the carriages:

As we attend to the train, we notice there's supper in one boxcar, but we just ate, so we're not pulled by that one. The laundry list is the next one, so we reflect for a moment on the blue towel hanging on the line to dry, but we wake up quite quickly to the present once again, as the next boxcar has someone in it meditating and we recall what we're doing. A few more boxcars go by with thoughts clearly recognized as thoughts. But, in the next one is a snarling lion chasing someone who looks like us. We stay with that one until it's way down the line to see if it gets us. We identify with that one because it 'means' something to us. We have an attachment to it. Then we notice we've missed all the other boxcars streaming by in the meantime and we let go of our fascination for the lion and bring our attention straight ahead into the present once again.

I love this description of the way our thoughts work while meditating. I also think it's a wonderful illustration of how they operate in general. Without the instruction or intention to keep our eyes straight ahead, how many of us realize that we have a choice? How many of us remember that we can simply focus on another carriage – the one with the supper or the laundry list in it? Or simply focus on looking straight into the present? How many of us realize that whatever we pay attention to can eat us up, whether it be a lion or a belief system?

Our negative beliefs are like snarling lions – they have us hooked. We are attached to them, so we focus on them and wrestle with them because we think that if we don't, they'll eat us. The irony is, the more we wrestle and fight, the more power we allow them. Stepping outside and observing our negative beliefs dissolves their power.

Rachel Dobson, Big Leaping from Sunday tabloid journalist to freelance journalist and property developer

I have what is commonly known as a scatterbrain. Never play word association with me, as the random results can be too scary. Since starting to meditate, I have freaked myself out further as I begin to explore how my mind can go from A to B via Pluto.

After leaving my job, I set up my own business, but fell into the pattern of doing exactly the same stuff I'd always done – but because I worked from home I could do the washing at the same time! It was pointless. I needed to be still and take stock. Unfortunately, this didn't mean heading to Thailand and booking into a fabulous spa, it meant making a habit of doing absolutely nothing for a small part of each and every day.

I started going to Hatha yoga classes at my gym – fantastic – lying flat on my back instead of pumping iron: easy. But the results are so much more obvious than spending weeks on the treadmill. The class has meditation at the beginning and end, and for me these are the most beneficial times. As a beginner, it's so tough to be still, but having the calming voice of a yoga teacher trained me into knowing how to relax and get into the flow of meditating.

At home, I sit on my bed, propped up by pillows with a thick pair of socks on! Once I'm comfortable, I concentrate on my breathing, in and out, gently through my nose. Every time I catch myself making a list of things to do that day, or having a chinwag with my bellowing old criticizing ego, or Inner Pessimist (as Suzy calls it), I come back to my breathing.

I reckon it takes, for me, a good 15–20 minutes to crack it. Around about then, my funny, loving, calm big sis with lovely, shiny, flowing hair – my version of the Inner Coach – tells me everything's okay, you'll have a great day, you did as best you could yesterday, get out there and enjoy yourself, love.

At first I ended up in tears when all I could hear was The Bitch of an ego banging on. Now I hear her stampeding through and think, 'Hiya, come to have your say?' Then I go back to my breathing in and out.

When I open my eyes, I feel refreshed, positive and focused. Then I let the good times flow – which they do – in abundance, if a little strangely. At the end of the day, I try to take a little time to acknowledge the good things that have happened, too.

When I meditate in the morning, whatever happens that day, if I catch myself stressing, I remember the breathing and that brings the feeling back. It's about me, what's happening to me inside, and how I'm reacting to external things. I'm the only one who can control this. I find the breathing is calming and helps me remember that. I don't sit cross-legged at my desk and hum, burn candles or play twangy mediation music. I just breathe in and out of my nose. It's like doing pelvic floor exercises, no one else knows you're doing it, you can do it anywhere, and the benefits are magnificent!

I recommend that you learn to meditate. Meditation helps us to step back from our negative beliefs and observe them, rather than constantly wrestle with our snarling lions. We can then choose to focus on our new positive beliefs, or even choose to simply stand on the sidelines and observe all our beliefs and thoughts

10 things you might be surprised to learn about meditation*

1. One study found that a group of 50 year olds who had been practising meditation for over five years showed a 12-year decrease in biological age.
2. Research shows that meditation is the most effective way to shake off addictions, such as to alcohol and cigarettes.

3. Studies have proved that meditation increases attention span, perception and memory, while improving verbal and analytical thinking.

4. Other studies have reported decreased requirements for medication among people who practise meditation, including reduced use of sleeping tablets and anti-depressants.

5. One five-year study found that among those who meditated regularly, there were 87 percent fewer hospitalizations for heart disease, 55 percent fewer tumours and 73 percent fewer throat and lung problems.

6. Many studies have shown that meditating regularly can reduce high blood pressure.

7. Meditating consistently has also been proven to decrease emotional problems, including depression, hostility and aggression.

8. An exhaustive study by the Swedish Natural Health Board found that psychiatric hospital admissions were much less common among people practising meditation than among the general public.

9. Based on research and clinical experience, meditation has been proven to reduce stress-related disorders such as migraine and anxiety.

10. In a controlled study on asthma, meditation was found to reduce the severity of symptoms.

*All the above refer to Transcendental Meditation.

Cultivating awareness is the key to sustaining the Big Leap. The more awareness you have, the quicker you can catch yourself before you dive into your old negative scripts. Awareness means you are not at the mercy of unconscious thought patterns but 'at choice'.

Petra has learned to meditate. She has gathered a great deal of evidence to show that she is a bright woman, and she now believes it. She believed it enough to resign from her job in television and take time off to travel the world. She may come back to it, she says, but only if she decides it's something she loves. 'I have changed the way I feel about myself, so I don't have to push myself any more. I feel like I have nothing to prove any more. It's incredibly liberating. I've taken some time out to get back in touch with what I want for myself, but the door is wide open. I feel the world is my oyster.'

Changing your self-beliefs will give you a sense of ease that will translate into how you approach your work, your social and family life, and your health. Letting go of negative beliefs will make a real difference to how you experience achieving your dreams.

Your Inner Pessimist is probably saying right now ...

'Good grief! You'll be wearing a kaftan and sandals next. Be careful. This sounds really cultish. She'll be asking you to give all your money to Father Christmas in the next chapter, just you wait. C'mon, let's get serious. You can't honestly believe that meditation will make any difference to your life. What, sitting down with your eyes closed? I think that's just a little excuse for a nap; don't you think that's a tad lazy? Where are you going to find the time to do that? Time for a reality check, methinks. Put the book down now. How about a glass of wine? Or shall we go to the pub? So much more fun than reading this dull book.'

What you need to be doing right now ...

Tune in to your Inner Coach. Write down in your journal what they have to say about all this.

The Big Baddie

'They sure knocked the stuffing out of you, didn't they?'

'Often people attempt to live their lives backwards; they try to have more things, or more money, in order to do more of what they want, so they will be happier. The way it actually works is the reverse. You must first be who you really are, then do what you need to do, in order to have what you want.'

— MARGARET YOUNG,
JAZZ SINGER (1891–1969)

Big Leap Step 5:   **THE BABY STEPS**

1. What is a scam?
2. Identify your scam
3. How to bust your scams
4. The transition

Now we're motoring! You've come out of denial, struggled through the void of fear, flown through la-la land, and all is well with the world. You know what you need to do to create the life you want. You're all set to make it happen – and then all of a sudden the Wicked Witch of the West turns up. In this step, the baddies are out to get you. Yes, you will face many obstacles – maybe a few with green faces. But the baddie you will have the most trouble with is … you! We can always find a reason not to do something, especially if it is challenging and difficult. This is where old behaviours can get in the way of your goals. I call them scams, and they give us the perfect excuse (in our own view, of course) to hold ourselves back and not take the plunge. Don't despair, you can beat the baddies. Just as Dorothy throws water at the Wicked Witch and she melts, you too can bust your scam.

Are you ready?

What you're probably thinking at Big Leap Step 5

- Big leap? Big heap of crap, more like.
- I'm too busy looking after the children to focus on this.
- I can't get my head around what I have to do.
- It will all go wrong, it always does for me.
- My husband/friend/dog has a broken leg; I have to help them first.
- Don't talk to me about big leaps, I've just found out my boyfriend is a woman!
- My vision isn't detailed enough yet. Just let me get it right first.
- Big leap into my bed. That's what I need.

What you're probably doing at Big Leap Step 5

- Sneering
- Sighing
- Farting loudly and pointing at the dog
- Giggling and simpering
- Moaning
- Flirting
- Drinking coffee and smoking cigarettes
- Shouting at people
- Slapping strangers and flouncing out the room

(If you don't understand, read on.)

You've come out of denial, you're working on your unmet needs, you've identified what you think you truly want in life, you've worked out what you'd have to believe to get it, and now in Big Leap Step 5, I want to stretch you a bit more and ask you to leap a little higher. I want you to get naked.

You know that nightmare where you go out and suddenly discover that people are pointing and laughing, because in fact you're stark naked and walking down the street in broad daylight? You know, the one where you try to run and hide, but you always end up flashing your bum? (What do you mean? You don't have that dream?) Well, perhaps you will after reading this chapter, because this step requires you to strip off a few layers.

Officially, it's about uncovering your 'scams', but the process can feel like peeling off all your clothes on a busy street so your goose-pimpled flesh is fully exposed to anyone who cares to look – which can make you feel rather uncomfortable.

Baby step 1:
What is a scam?

We create scams when we don't know how to get our emotional needs satisfied in a healthy way and when our belief systems about ourselves and life are essentially negative. Scams are:

- A cluster of unmet needs and beliefs that have evolved into an 'identity'.
- A 'costume' in which we dress up to present ourselves to the world (and perhaps even ourselves).
- The emotional protection we created in childhood to help us survive in the grown-up world.

Our scams are essentially the systems we created to keep ourselves safe as children. The Inner Pessimist loves these kinds of systems. But scams can become very inefficient, and, by the time we've reached adulthood, they're probably very much out of date. After all, when we are no longer children, we don't need a child's response to a situation.

As a child, you might have made a decision to become the class joker because you were bullied in the playground. The scam was useful then, because it meant the other kids laughed at you rather than thumped you. But 30 years on, behaving like the joker in the office is probably seriously holding you back. Your 'silly antics' might make people like you, but they don't get you anywhere in your career.

So now it's time to decide to drop that old behaviour in favour of something more appropriate and reflective of who you are as an adult. If you need to, you can learn some new ways to get your need for protection met – or maybe you can decide that you just don't need to protect yourself any more. After all, you're no longer in the playground, and you can choose other ways to deal with any bullies you might encounter. It's quite a liberating idea. Let me tell you about my own little scam so you get an idea of how they work – or don't work!

My little scam

My favourite scam used to be 'poor, brave me'. I was the world's favourite martyr. I did everything for everyone else – I was a giving friend, a dutiful daughter, and a wife who supported her husband emotionally (and financially for a while). How was I? 'Fine, if a bit tired/stressed/worn out,' I'd say with a little sigh.

I'd set up this scam in childhood. This is how I got love and attention as a child. At some point, I'd come to the conclusion that love wasn't unconditional, and I would have to do something to receive it. The way I chose to get the love I wanted was to be a giver and a martyr. I'd clean the house for my parents; I wouldn't stay out late because I didn't want them to worry; I was the sweet, giving one of the family. I was lavished with praise, love and attention for playing this little scam. It was glorious. Everyone would say how lovely I was. No one ever criticized me or said anything bad about me because I was doing everything 'right'. I was there for everyone, was 'sweet and kind' and 'only trying to help'. I got what I needed. It was a fantastic scam to set up, if I do say so myself.

However, 30 years on, it wasn't working for me any more. I was twitchy with resentment. I was constantly screening my answering machine because friends were always ringing to dump their problems on me. 'No one ever listens to me,' I'd sigh. I resented my husband (now my ex) for having the freedom and money to go off and follow his dreams even though I couldn't follow mine; but I'd never say anything, I'd just stew inwardly. 'You go on, darling, and be happy. I'll just sit here and be miserable.' I know, nothing as revolting as the smell of burning martyr, is there?

I'd find myself working all the hours of the day because I didn't want to say 'no' to my bosses. I wanted everyone to like me and to think I was incredibly hardworking and dynamic. Predictably, I began to lose my energy. I started to use stimulants like coffee and cigarettes to help me get through the day. I was constantly exhausted, which meant that I got to sigh all the more. I still got to be a martyr, but eventually, I was fed up with it. It was costing me big time – my relationship, my health, my sanity. 'Time for some scambusting,' my coach suggested.

Baby step 2:
Identify your scam

Scambusting? We'll get to that in a minute, but first,
let's take a look at some of the more popular scams of the
hundreds that we can play. This will help you in the
essential step of identifying your scam.

It's not the most pleasant part of the Big Leap journey.
Believe me, if you're normal, you don't want to own up to
a scam. To be honest, it's downright embarrassing. In fact,
many people can get very angry when they read the
descriptions below.

Some of us so highly identify with our scam that we think
we are our scam. If we stop playing it, then who are we?
We will protect our scams at all costs because we feel they
protect us. We have constructed them to emotionally
survive our childhood, and if that protection barrier starts
to wobble, we can become very defensive.

It can feel frightening to suddenly see your scam in black
and white. Because I highly identified with mine, I felt
like someone had taken away my personality. If I wasn't
the martyr or people-pleaser, then who was I? How
would I react, how would I act, what would I do with
the rest of my life? I'd been playing the people-pleaser
since childhood – how was I supposed to behave now?

So be prepared to react quite strongly when you read the
descriptions of some of the more typical scams that we
play, along with the possible unmet needs they fulfil and
the belief systems they may be trying to compensate for.
If your scam still serves you well and is costing you very
little, then you probably won't find this section very

useful. If, for example, you have constructed 'the Joker' scam and made a successful career as a comedian, you probably won't want to start looking at changing it. Your scam is still working for you.

However, for those of us struggling with a behaviour that has begun to hold us back, you may find the following useful.

The scam: the Cynic

You are always cynical, disbelieving anything other than what you think is right. A permanent sneer is etched on your face.

The most likely thing for a Cynic to say:
'Yeah, right!'

The most likely thing for a Cynic to do:
Snort derisively

Possible unmet need:
Protection

Possible pay-offs:
It keeps you safe, as you don't have to come out of your comfort zone. It's easier to sneer at and mock other people's efforts than actually dare to do something differently yourself.

Possible belief systems you are compensating for:
'You can't trust the world. You can't trust life. You can't trust others.'

Possible costs:
You find it difficult to create intimate relationships and you feel lonely. You make enemies easily. You're not that

likeable, although some people think cynicism is cool, so you may be popular with certain groups of people – like journalists.

The scam: the Martyr

You are a people-pleaser that does everything for everyone else and quietly resents it. People generally take the Martyr for granted and do not feel grateful for their help.

The most likely thing for a Martyr to say:

'Don't worry about me.' Sigh. 'I'll just stay in and do that for you.' Sigh.

The most likely thing for a Martyr to do:

Sigh quietly

Possible unmet needs:

To be loved; approved of: needed; to feel secure

Possible pay-offs:

You make yourself indispensable in everybody's life so no one will leave you. You don't have to risk failing or coming out of your comfort zone because you spend all your energy sorting out other people's lives.

Possible belief systems you are compensating for:

'I am not enough. Love is conditional. I must do a + b + c to be loved.'

Possible costs:

You're constantly exhausted. You become bitter and resentful. Your children never leave home. You die never having achieved what you wanted to achieve.

The scam: the Joker

You constantly laugh and joke. You keep everyone around you laughing all the time by playing lots of silly tricks at work and at home.

The most likely thing for a Joker to say:
'Have you heard the one about …?'

The most likely thing for a Joker to do:
Fart loudly, and then point at the dog

Possible unmet needs:
To be liked; to be safe

Possible pay-offs:
You never have to be honest about how you're really feeling. You never have to make yourself vulnerable. People generally like you as long as you don't take it too far. You're usually the most popular person in a group.

Possible belief systems you are compensating for:
'No one will love me if I'm just me. Everyone is a threat who I need to disarm. I will be attacked if I don't protect myself.'

Possible costs:
You never talk about how you really feel, so you can feel lonely and isolated. People don't take you seriously at work, which can cost you financially as well as emotionally.

The scam: the Flake

You play the 'dizzy blonde' who just can't get her life together. You're usually in debt and have relationship traumas, but you're almost proud of the fact. Family and friends smile at you indulgently.

The most likely thing for a Flake to say:
'Oh, well, you know what I'm like!'

The most likely thing for a Flake to do:
Giggle inappropriately

Possible unmet needs:
Protection; to be looked after; to be loved

Possible pay-offs:
You don't have to risk taking responsibility for your life.
You get looked after by others and get lots of attention.
You are usually greatly loved by others because you
don't threaten them. People love to hear your disaster
stories because it makes them feel better about their
own lives.

Possible belief systems you are compensating for:
'I must appear unthreatening or I will be attacked. I'm
not clever/good/beautiful enough to get what I want. I am
clever/good/beautiful enough to get what I want, but if
I show people this, they will attack me.'

Possible costs:
Your life is in constant crisis, which can be pretty stressful
at times, especially if you don't have your usual team in
place to rescue you. If you want to live comfortably, you
have to hook up with someone wealthy (parents or
partner usually) as you'll never be able to afford the
good life on your own.

The scam: the Misery Magnet
You're always unhappy and constantly moaning.

The most likely thing for a Misery Magnet to say:
'Life is hard and then you die.'

The most likely thing for a Misery Magnet to do:
Look utterly miserable

Possible unmet needs:
To be nurtured; to be listened to; to be soothed

Possible pay-offs:
You get a lot of attention from people who love you because they want you to be happy. They are constantly trying to help you or make a situation better. You can get attention by joining a new group, as they also try to 'fix' your misery.

Possible belief systems you are compensating for:
'I am invisible and will not be loved unless I have a problem.'

Possible costs:
Eventually those who love you get fed up with your moaning and may leave you. In a group situation, after being the centre of attention for a while, people soon lose interest as they realize you are determined not to be cheered up. You can become very unpopular and therefore isolated and lonely. (Unless you hook up with a Martyr or a Rescuer.)

The scam: the Rescuer

You spend your life rescuing people or animals and generally focusing on lost causes. Usually you will seek a relationship with an alcoholic, depressive or a Misery Magnet. Generally you get more joy out of helping people than the Martyr.

The most likely thing for a Rescuer to say:
'Let me do that for you.'

The most likely thing for a Rescuer to do:
Tap dance and laugh to make everything better

Possible unmet needs:
To be needed; loved; accepted

Possible pay-offs:
You always have a role to play in a group situation.
You're generally respected and admired by others. You're
seen as being a 'good' person. You receive the grateful
thanks of those you rescue (if not, you become a Martyr).

Possible belief systems you are compensating for:
'My needs are not important. I must always meet others'
needs before my own if I am to be loved and accepted.'

Possible costs:
It can be exhausting. You tend to slump in a heap at the end
of the day. You never have the time or energy to sort out
your own life, because you're too busy cheering up everyone
else. You're generally unfulfilled and dissatisfied with life.
You worry constantly about others and how they are and
constantly have to ring people just to check they're okay.

The scam: the Rebel

You hate any kind of authority and constantly rebel. You
always hate your boss, whatever job you're in.

The most likely thing for a Rebel to say:
'Fuck 'em!'

The most likely thing for a Rebel to do:
Smoke cigarettes in a non-smoking area

Possible unmet needs:
To stand out; to control your destiny

Possible pay-offs:
You feel special and different. You get a kick out of not conforming, which can buy you admiration in some circles. You can be quite creative in finding new ways to do things (in an attempt to be different), so you could be very successful at running your own business.

Possible belief systems you are compensating for:
'I am not special. If I'm like everyone else, I will disappear/not be loved/noticed.'

Possible costs:
You're constantly battling or fighting with people or organizations, which can be wearing for you and those around you. You might indulge in things that aren't good for your health, such as cigarettes, alcohol, and unprotected sex, which can cost you greatly in the long run.

The scam: the Victim
Something terrible is always happening to you. You're either being victimized, bullied, sacked, mugged, losing your purse, getting ill (again), being cheated on by your partner or being badly treated by your friends.

The most likely thing for a Victim to say:
'It's not my fault!'

The most likely thing for a Victim to do:
Recount the latest list of horrors

Possible unmet needs:
To be listened to; looked after; loved; soothed

Possible pay-offs:
You do not have to take responsibility for yourself. You can be passive and wait to be rescued by someone else

(although you resist this with all your might). You get lots of sympathy and attention. You don't have to come out of your comfort zone and risk failure or rejection.

Possible belief systems you are compensating for:
'People don't love me and it's my fault because I'm unlovable.'

Possible costs:
You live your life in the twilight zone of misery. You never experience real joy. People eventually get sick of your misery and start to move away, wondering if you're either cursed or you're bringing it on yourself. You can be quite lonely.

The scam: the Drama Queen
Your life is a constant whirl of dramatic scenes – huge fights with your boss, visits to the hospital with cancer scares that turn out to be in-grown hairs, and constant high drama in your love life. Your would-be partners always turn out to be commitment-phobes.

The most likely thing for a Drama Queen to say:
'Oh. My. God. You will never guess what happened to me today!'

The most likely thing for a Drama Queen to do:
Slap someone and flounce out of a room

Possible unmet needs:
Attention; to be adored; to be acclaimed

Possible pay-offs:
You are always the centre of attention. If you're not there, people are always talking about you. You get a lot of energy and buzz from constantly living in this field of high drama.

Possible belief systems you are compensating for:
'I am nothing. I am nobody.'

Possible costs:
You never get real or lead an emotionally healthy life.
You can't form good, stable relationships. You tend to be
surrounded by fellow Drama Queens, Rescuers or
Martyrs who will listen to your tales of woe and try to
rescue you, or offer to go with you to the STD clinic.

The scam: the Adrenaline Addict

Generally you're a procrastinator who leaves everything
to the last minute. Everything is always done in a rush
and with much suffering. You use coffee or cigarettes to
give you the energy to keep going.

The most likely thing for an Adrenaline Addict to say:
'I'll do it tomorrow.'

The most likely thing for an Adrenaline Addict to do:
Drink ten cups of coffee a day

Possible unmet needs:
To be approved of; to be valued for who you are

Possible pay-offs:
You get a lot done, very quickly. You tend to be very
'high energy' most of the time and can be very dynamic
and successful in your career.

Possible belief systems you are compensating for:
'I am not good enough, I will fail and everyone will laugh.'

Possible costs:
You can push yourself so hard that you end up collapsing
and falling ill. If you're using adrenaline as a source of

energy, it's usually because you're doing tasks or a career
that you don't enjoy, so you have to force yourself to do it.
Being an Adrenaline Addict usually means you're not
living the life you really want to live.

The scam: the Perfectionist

You are a control freak. Everything has to be done to your
very high standards, otherwise it's completely wrong.
You'd rather do it all yourself than let someone else mess it
up. You're the boss who has to oversee every last detail or
the mother who won't let anyone look after her child.

The most likely thing for a Perfectionist to say:

'You're doing it wrong. Give it to me.'

The most likely thing for a Perfectionist to do:

Shout at people – a lot

Possible unmet needs:

To be in control; to be safe; to be right; to be in charge

Possible pay-offs:

You are indispensable. As you are always in control, you
don't have to trust others. You can control your
environment, which makes you feel safe and secure.

Possible belief systems you are compensating for:

'I have to earn my place in the world, otherwise I will get
hurt/attacked. I can trust only myself.'

Possible costs:

You have to work 24/7, which will cause you to burn out.
You are the boss from hell and are disliked because you
don't encourage people, just criticize them. No one can do
it as well as you can, so you have to do everything in your
company or home.

The scam: the Vamp/the Stud

You play the sexual lothario/temptress in every situation.
You cannot finish a sentence without a double entendre.
You seduce and manipulate people with your sexual wiles.

The most likely thing for a Vamp/Stud to say:

'I can't stop staring at your lips.'

The most likely thing for a Vamp/Stud to do:

Stare at your lips

Possible unmet needs:

To be noticed; in control; liked; loved

Possible pay-offs:

You have a role to play on every occasion. Because you
know how to charm and seduce people, you are popular
with strangers. Your self-esteem is regularly massaged –
as is your body.

Possible belief systems you are compensating for:

'I am unlovable. I have to make them like me before they
reject me.'

Possible costs:

As you get older, you become more unpopular and 'sad',
since you cannot seduce with your looks any more. If
you're rejected, you can quickly become very unhappy.
You constantly change groups of friends since your only
way of communicating with people is to seduce them, and
then you have to move on to new pastures. This can be
unsettling and isolating. You may indulge in unprotected
sex and put your health at risk.

You may not completely identify with any of the scams
above, but you might recognize echoes of your behaviour

in them. Don't fall into the trap of pointing out to your friends and family what scams they're currently playing. You might think it's the perfect party game to play, but it isn't, trust me. Just focus on yourself.

Rachel Dobson, Big Leaping from Sunday tabloid journalist to freelance journalist and property developer

If you really can't see the scam you've got running and you're feeling brave, let your best friend or partner read this chapter, and let them tell you! It's much easier to identify other people's scams than your own. Only try this if you're feeling very brave, though, and have a very loving best friend or partner. Never, ever show this chapter to anyone who could use it against you!

I won't kid you here – identifying your scam is not a pleasant process. It can be quite emotional when you begin to piece together the possible belief systems and unmet needs that you have been compensating for all your life. It can be terrifying, too. These behaviours, our scams, serve us when we're not aware of what we're doing, but as soon as you spot the scam, you have nowhere to hide.

However, no matter how horrific it is to discover what little scams you have been running in your life, it can also be a relief. It explains all sorts of weird behaviour that you might have indulged in and also helps you understand why you've done it.

Usually we're only motivated to start busting our scam if the costs outweigh the pay-offs. If this applies to you, try this three-step scambusting exercise, which may help guide you to find a healthier and more efficient way of getting what you need.

Ready to leap

Exercise: SCAMBUSTING

Part 1

Identify your scam. Write your answers in your journal.

- What is your scam?
- When you're in full scam mode, what sort of things do you find yourself saying?
- When you're in full scam mode, what sort of things do you find yourself doing?
- Be very honest. What are the pay-offs for this behaviour?
- What is it costing you?
- Are you willing to give up your scam?

Part 2

Now identify your unmet needs. What do you really need? Write your answers in your journal and if you're struggling to answer this question, ask yourself:

- What do you really want? If I could wave a magical wand and give you three wishes that would allow you to create your ideal life, what would they be? (e.g. Lots of money? A loving partner? A private jet?)
- Next, ask yourself what these things will get you (e.g. Financial security? Love? Freedom? Privacy?)
- Finally, ask yourself what you really need to feel happy. What do you need to feel expanded, generous, at one with the world?

Part 3

Finally, identify the negative belief system at the root of your scam. Using the process we explored in Big Leap Step 4, create a new belief system that will support healthier and more resourceful behaviour. Then start to take the steps in baby step 3 to create evidence to prove that this new belief system is true.

Baby step 3:
How to bust your scams

Busting your scams means taking a good look at the unmet needs and limiting beliefs that have held you back for so long and putting in place new beliefs and actions. It sounds easy, but this process really challenges your commitment to change.

You have to change how you look at life, what you believe you can do, and who you believe you can be. This is the way to make your la-la land a reality in your life.

You may need to take a deep breath, but you know you can do it – it's just a matter of being vigilant and determined to succeed.

Busting the Cynic
The new belief:
  'I can trust others.'

The scambuster:
  Instead of sneering cynically to protect yourself, you could listen to what others say. Perhaps do your own research and make an informed decision as to whether or not to trust someone.

The baby step:
  Don't automatically assume that others are not to be trusted. Be willing to be open; you can still protect yourself by doing the research. This will help you build evidence that others/life can be trusted sometimes.

Busting the Martyr and the Rescuer

The new belief:

'I am loved for who I am, not for what I do for others. My needs are important.'

The scambuster:

Instead of doing things for others to try to win their approval, start focusing on your own needs. Ask yourself, 'What do I need here?'

The baby step:

Start to ask friends and loved ones for what you need, whether it be for help or for a hug when you're feeling down. This starts to build the evidence that you don't have to do anything to be loved.

Busting the Joker

The new belief:

'I can just be me and people will like me and not attack me.'

The scambuster:

Instead of immediately going into your full-blown comedy routine when you're in the company of others, start to share how you really think and feel about something – without adding a punchline!

The baby step:

If you're with people who know you very well, they may be expecting you to be funny, so perhaps only try out these different behaviours with new people until you build your confidence.

Busting the Flake

The new belief:

'I can shine and people won't attack me.'

The scambuster:

Stop giggling and hiding your talents and take yourself seriously.

The baby step:

Join a new social group in which it would be appropriate for you to behave like the intelligent, incisive and likeable person you are (e.g. a book club). Practise being your most brilliant self. Social convention will usually stop anyone from attacking you, which will give you a place to let your brilliance out of the bag in a safe environment.

Busting the Misery Magnet and the Drama Queen

The new belief:

'I am loved and listened to. I am heard.'

The scambuster:

Talk to your loved ones about your unmet needs. Explain how important it is to you to be listened to and for your feelings to be heard and acknowledged. Coach them how to listen to you and reflect back how you are feeling without offering how to 'fix' you. When you start to feel that you don't need to have a problem or drama in order to command attention, the old behaviour will begin to fade.

The baby step:

Set up a formal time and space to be 'listened to' weekly. Set ground rules – you must not be interrupted, there must be no judgements, you don't want to be fixed, you just want lots of hugs and acknowledgement at the end of your 'session'.

Busting the Rebel and the Vamp/Stud

The new belief:

'I don't have to fight/seduce anyone to justify my place in the world. I can just be, and others will notice and love me.'

The scambuster:

Instead of focusing on your impact on others, bring your attention to your own needs and wants. Figure out what you actually want to do with your time. What interests you? What do you do naturally? What do you enjoy doing?

The baby step:

Create a 30-day 'golden glow' project based on what you love doing as opposed to what you think will get you attention.

Busting the Victim

The new belief:

'I am lovable.'

The scambuster:

Take responsibility. As long as you are blaming others and the world for your misfortunes, you will never be able to bust your scam.

The baby step:

Be extremely compassionate with yourself. Explore the idea that your basic self-belief systems are creating your current reality. Changing your belief system will change your reality. Work with a therapist on healing childhood wounds and start to build evidence that you are lovable.

Busting the Adrenaline Addict

The new belief:

'I am good enough.'

The scambuster:

Start cataloguing concrete evidence from your past that proves to you that you are good enough – from your qualifications to what your best friend has to say about you. Write it all down in your journal.

The baby step:

When you feel the fear of failure, talk it through with a friend instead of spiralling into adrenaline-fuelled behaviour. Tune into your Inner Coach and listen to what they have to say.

Busting the Perfectionist

The new belief:

'I am loved unconditionally.'

The scambuster:

Learn to question your own set of internal rules about what is right and wrong. If you put your rules aside for a second and take a step back, what do you really feel, want and need?

The baby step:

Allow yourself to make minor errors – not create the perfect cakes/documents/artwork – and discover that the world does not fall down around your ears. Notice that you are likeable even though you're not perfect.

Get some therapy!

Because our scams are often compensations for certain needs that weren't met in childhood, sometimes it is useful to work with a therapist on healing any wounds that are still gaping and oozing. A trained professional can create a compassionate space for you to vent your feelings and allow the healing process to begin.

You may need therapy if:

- You cannot think about your childhood without feeling angry, hurt and upset.
- You cannot stop crying after reading this chapter about scams.
- You feel you can never forgive the people who did this to you.
- You want to cut your parents/grandparents/so-called responsible adults out of your life forever.
- You have already cut your parents/grandparents/so-called responsible adults out of your life and hate them with a boiling passion.

Baby step 4:
The transition

Scambusting cracks your shell and lets the 'real you' emerge. Yes, you can feel very vulnerable and 'naked' at first, but it is also incredibly liberating. The real you is the one that isn't performing or making great efforts to get something. You just turn up and say what you have to say. You don't have to rehearse, you don't have to perform, and you'll notice that your behaviour begins to change. You become less poised, less tight and more relaxed and easy with yourself and others. You're in touch with what you really want and need, and you can ask for it honestly rather than twisting yourself into a strange scam-like shape to get it.

However, there is a transition that you have to go through first. We have adopted our scam for a reason. Bust your scam – and then what? Your fears of being unlovable, unsafe and unacceptable rush to the fore. 'Protect yourself, protect yourself!' screams your Inner Pessimist. 'You don't know who you are, you don't know how to react, you feel lost and scared of being rejected by others.'

This transition is not helped by the fact that other people may react negatively to the new you at first (after all, you've just changed roles as well as the rules, and they may not like it). 'What do you mean you're not going to rescue me/flirt with me/collude with my cynicism/smoke with me behind the shed anymore?' You may have to redefine your relationships. Be honest and tell them your discoveries about yourself. Again, try not to point the finger and say, 'Well, if you weren't such a Misery Magnet, I wouldn't have to rescue you so much.' We don't know what is going on for other people. It's not up to us to bust anyone else's scam. Just stick with your own.

Rachel Dobson, Big Leaping from Sunday tabloid journalist to freelance journalist and property developer

I have never felt that I matched up to any of my friends or colleagues since as long as I can remember. But I was always popular because I was a laugh. When I was a teenager, I would drink the most, date gorgeous boys and always, always be up for a laugh. Booking a holiday? Dobbo will come. Having a party? Get Dobbo the icebreaker along.

Starting college, I got along with everyone and anyone. I never intimidated anyone – I was always the one to ask the stupid question, wear inappropriate clothes and do something for a joke. I had friends, was comfortable, unchallenged and enjoying myself.

Because I hid behind the mask of being a 'divvy', I never flourished. I never went for the job I really, really wanted. I never believed I would get it – after all I was the girl who made everyone else feel like Einstein, so how could I possibly work at that level?

So the pay-off was that I paddled along in easy, junior positions, having a laugh, making friends, looking like I had a successful career. The cost was that I wasn't proud of myself. I didn't feel I achieved anything. I was frustrated and unchallenged and resented people thinking I was less clever than I am. In fact, I have a first-class honours degree – something only one other person on my course had achieved – but because it's not from Cambridge I took it off my CV. Any employer who's ever seen my CV thinks I landed my first job because of my secretarial qualifications – at least I didn't have to live up to anything.

Eventually, this started to gnaw away at me. I felt bitter and hated myself for not being brave enough to live up to what I thought I could. People believed I really was a thicko because my work was terrible. I wasn't interested in it. I just went through the motions – a cheery good morning to everyone every day. Nobody guessed this role wasn't my life's ambition.

Working through the Big Leap exercises, it turned out that my big need was for acclaim, which was quite a surprise to me. I was also looking for the freedom to be myself, the security to feel comfortable, lots of love and lots of fun, too – that's still one of my key needs.

So I left my job and set up my own business, and I've never been so challenged in my whole life. I've had many, many moments when I've thought, who the hell do I think I am? What am I trying to do here? I spiral into meltdown and sob. Then I have to pick myself up and think: baby steps, baby steps. Thirty years of doing it one way (gulp – the waste!) has left its mark, but luckily that's not impossible to change.

When I have a 'moment', I remind myself of past victories and dwell on them. I have a diary with five little things to do each day – ranging from sending an email to reading an article. I tick them off – happy at having done them, but not caring what the outcome of those actions is. Most of all, I remember that it's meant to be enjoyable, too. So I go out and have some fun – even if that just means rollerblading to the newsagents. I couldn't do that when I was stuck at work everyday, could I?

The hard work has been in identifying the scam. Once you have, the work can begin. Slowly, bit by bit, you start to recognize your old patterns of behaviour and start choosing a new way of being.

10 ways you know you're in transition

1. You suddenly don't know how to talk to your friends or partner.
2. 'I don't know who I am any more' is your favourite phrase.
3. You feel unsure about how to react in new situations – you don't have a comfortable 'routine' you fall into.
4. If a crisis hits, you find yourself falling completely into your old scam and rescuing/flirting/snarling your way out of it.
5. You find yourself at a loss when someone asks you, 'What do you want to do tonight?'
6. You question your motives about why you want to be around certain people. Is it because you really like them, or is it because you want to seduce, rescue or control them?

7. You find yourself having spectacular rows with your friends, family and partner.
8. You don't go out as much.
9. You find yourself bored and restless.
10. Sometimes, you feel so sick with fear, you want to blot it all out and go out drinking/watch back-to-back films on TV/sleep all day.

The no-judgement rule

Just as with our negative beliefs, our scams tend to hang around. In times of stress, my Martyr complex can quickly enter stage right, huffing and puffing as she climbs the stairs. 'Okay …' she sighs. 'Who do you want me to help now?' I know how to operate with my scam in place. I feel protected. It gets me loved – albeit at a price. When working on our self-development, we often feel that once we've 'seen' something about the way we operate, we're 'cured'. So we believe that once our scam is busted, we'll live happily ever after from that moment on. That's not been my experience. It's not about 'getting rid' of the scam, but rather being aware of it, and then choosing to do something different in the moment. It's an ongoing process.

That's why we have to put a no-judgement rule in place. When we see our scamming behaviour, either for the first time or 10 years down the line, the easiest reaction is to judge ourselves. When I first identified my Martyr scam, I had a field day. I felt I'd been behaving like an emotional prostitute: constantly pleasing other people for what they would 'pay' me in their affection and approval. I look back now and squirm at the ridiculous extremes I went to. I practically put my whole career on hold for my ex-husband so he could be successful (anything, anything, just please love me). I even promised a complete stranger a room to rent in my house because I sensed she didn't like me, but I knew she needed somewhere to live (I ended up taking her messages and doing her washing). I once paid a £300 bar bill – the whole evening's drinks for all our friends – because I'd got a little drunk, upset a friend and wanted to make sure she still liked me. Then I quietly and bitterly resented it.

When I began to catalogue the costs of my scam – not only emotionally, but financially, too – I wanted to weep and rage. I judged myself for being stupid, pathetic, a prostitute for approval. But judging yourself, as I discovered, simply makes it worse. It makes you feel ashamed and utterly self-loathing, which doesn't help at all. In fact, it can just be another way to keep you obsessing about your inner dramas rather than getting on with the real task of creating a life that you adore. It's much easier to keep judging yourself because that keeps you stuck. You don't have to come out of your comfort zone and start to experiment with supportive and healthy new behaviours, which, admittedly, can feel challenging, strange and scary.

You need to have the utmost compassion for yourself during the process of busting your scams and keeping them busted. After all, you were only doing what you thought was best at the time you created them. You weren't consciously playing these scams; most likely you created them because you were too scared to do anything else. It takes courage and a lot of humility to identify them and decide to do something about them. It can take moment-by-moment awareness at times, but the more you are yourself, the easier life becomes.

10 ways to know that your scam is busted

1. You tell the truth.
2. You no longer screen your telephone calls.
3. Life becomes boring for about three months, and then peaceful.
4. You spend time with people you adore and who adore you – and laugh a lot.
5. You get absolute clarity about what the next step is for you, and you can't understand why you didn't see it before.
6. You no longer procrastinate, but get things done quickly and efficiently.
7. You are kinder to others and to yourself.
8. You stop trying to get your point across and listen more.
9. You are happy to spend time alone.
10. New friends, who you really like, come into your life.

Your Inner Pessimist is probably saying right now ...

'Don't get naked, your bum will frighten people. Are you insane? Drop your scam? How will you survive in the world without it? You'll be lost and miserable. No one will like you if you don't rescue/flirt/sneer/help. You know what? You're right. You are unloveable, and unacceptable, and you're right, you can't trust others. They'll just stab you in the back, you know they will. You don't know who you are and it's probably best it stays that way.'

What you need to be doing right now ...

Tune in to your Inner Coach. Write down in your journal what she has to say about all this.

The Big Low

'I'm frightened, Auntie Em! I'm frightened!'

*'However long the night,
the dawn will break.'*

— AFRICAN PROVERB

Big Leap Step 6:   THE BABY STEPS

1. Tell us about the money, honey
2. The F-word
3. Heartbreak
4. Surrender!

Prepare yourself, you are about to embark on an unpleasant part of the journey. In fact, this step is usually the worst. No, it's always the worst. This is your rock bottom moment. It is where you face failure, and your fears come to roost in your bedroom and fly down and peck at your brain in the middle of the night. Your back is against the wall, you feel you have no options left. You have a moment, day or week of total despair. It can be about money, if your survival needs are not met. Or you might lose faith in yourself, in your idea of ever achieving your dream. You lose your hope, your love, your everything. Yes, it's a dark place. Your dark night of the soul. But don't panic; even though this is a painful place to be, it's also where transformation happens. It's when you find a way; you see the light at the end of the tunnel. Without reaching rock bottom, we can't make the leap. Rock bottom is your springboard to transformation. Really. Don't leave me now.

What you're probably thinking at Big Leap Step 6

- I'm lost.
- I've lost everyone and everything I ever cared about.
- I'm worse off than I've ever been.
- Someone please rescue me, I have no energy left to rescue myself.
- The dream is over.
- Why did I bother?
- I'm back here again.
- I miss you.
- I hate this day.

What you're probably doing at Big Leap Step 6

- Weeping quietly.
- Lying in the metaphorical gutter.
- Lying in a real gutter.
- Hiding in shame from everyone you know.
- Drinking alcohol/feeding your face/smoking/doing anything you can to numb the pain.
- Sleeping as much as possible so you don't have to wake up and face what is happening.

I know you'll be feeling pretty low right now but this is actually the most profound and transformational moment in the whole Big Leap journey. This is the moment that you get to learn the biggest lessons and turn your life around. Let's go.

Baby step 1:
Tell us about the money, honey

Lack of money can often be the problem that brings most Big Leaps to a grinding halt. Money is linked not only to our emotional needs for security, but also to our survival needs. All the meditating and visualizing in the world won't pay the bills or put food on the table. When we are constantly focusing on our vanishing bank accounts, it feels impossible, painful and terrifying to even think about making the Big Leap.

I wish I'd known all this when I made my Big Leap. I must admit that I'm rather an optimist. I had trained to be a coach, spent a fortune on my letterhead, bought a headset for my phone and then sat like a lemon and waited for it to ring. It didn't. The bills began to flood in and my debts stacked up, as did my anxiety levels. Three months in and I was panicking, 'But this is my dream job. I've had my bingo moment. Why isn't it working?' I felt twitchy, envious of others. I felt closed down, strained, desperate. I would have coached anyone with a pulse. No one volunteered.

Are you surprised? People can smell fear and desperation. When you have unmet survival needs, you are going nowhere fast. It becomes a downward spiral. Because what you focus on expands, the more you focus on the lack, the more lack you attract.

My ex-husband started huffing and puffing in the background as the debts began to seep through to the joint account. 'Don't you believe in me?' I screamed. 'Do you believe in yourself?' asked my coach.

If our belief systems create our reality, what belief was creating this current reality? When I explored this with my coach, it was my 'not good enough' stuff floating to the surface again. I had just qualified as a coach; how did I know I was good enough? What evidence did I have? Not a lot. To build my belief systems, I had to really 'know' that I was a good coach. In order to know this, I had to build my business and profile so that people could contact me. This process takes time. I needed to find part-time work in the meantime so that I wasn't reliant on my coaching work to support me financially.

As Big Leaper Nicky advises, it can take more time than we estimate to create the life we want. If we want to enjoy the journey, we need to take the pressure off ourselves as we build the evidence to support our new belief systems and build our new lives.

The situation that strikes dread into my heart is when a client, inspired and full of enthusiasm after completing their vision and wild-eyed from their bingo moment, tells me that they resigned from their job that morning. With no money coming in, that enthusiasm and inspiration will drain away as quickly as water draining from a bath.

You need to be able to support yourself financially on your Big Leap journey if you want to have a pleasant ride. This may mean staying in your full-time job and retraining in the evenings and weekends, or waiting to emigrate until you have money saved.

Nicky was made redundant, so she rented out her house while she stayed with friends and built up her business. Even though Andrew took the Big Leap and travelled to Hong Kong without savings, he owned a flat in London, and he knew that if things got really bad he could always sell it.

Yes, it takes a leap of faith to make the Big Leap, but it's a lot less scary if you create a safety net. Don't shy away from the financial or practical issues of working out exactly how are you going to do it.

Ready to leap

Exercise: GETTING PRACTICAL

Try answering these questions in your journal.

- How much money do you need to make your Big Leap?
- How do you intend to finance it?
- What will have to believe about yourself to finance it?
- How could you prevent financial worries from sabotaging your Big Leap?
- What does your Inner Coach have to say about money?
- What five baby steps could you make this week to create a sound financial plan?
- What practical steps can you take to start putting this plan into action? (e.g. moonlight in order to save £100 a week for the next three months; investigate part-time jobs; get a student loan; talk to the Citizen's Advice Bureau.

Nicky Hambleton-Jones, Big Leaping from management consultant to celebrity fashion stylist

Set yourself up to succeed by overestimating the time it will take. If you think it'll take one month to set up a bank loan, allow four months. If you think it will take two months to set up a business alliance, allow six months. Everything takes much longer than you think it will.

Sometimes I felt like giving up because I'd have days and days without one phone call. Then something amazing would happen, like an article would be published in a newspaper and I'd be inundated. But you can't rely on a new business for all your income. It took me two years before I started earning a decent wage. My turnover for the first year was £3,000! At one point, I rented out my flat and was living in friends' houses to save money. I also had to get a part-time job. That was my saviour. Most businesses fail because of cash flow in the early days, so make sure you have some other source of income. It's also very isolating when you start your own business, so a part-time job is great just for the company.

Baby step 2:
The F-word

When you're on the Big Leap journey, fear of failure is a biggie. It is the one fear that the Inner Pessimist doesn't have to shout about. One little whisper is enough to stop us dead in our tracks. Our Big Leap journey is about aligning our whole lives with our passions, fulfilling our purpose – so where do you go from here if you fail spectacularly? Wouldn't it be terrible to get this far and discover your Inner Pessimist is right? You would feel such a fool to have tried. Yet it's about more than the fear of feeling foolish. It would be like witnessing the death of your dreams.

Failure. It's the big F-word. Most of us have been burned or branded by it, whether as a child, teenager or adult. It's hideous. So when my coach told me that there was no such thing as failure, but simply 'learning experiences', I had to disagree. No such thing as failure? Fear of failing had kept me up too many nights to let this one pass without a fight.

How would our worlds be different if we weren't scared of failure? How would life be different if failure was seen as one of the most valuable things we could do? How would life be different if we took pride in listing our failures? What would it be like if failure wasn't a full stop, but the springboard for leaping to a whole new level? How would our lives be different if we brought up our children with a healthy respect for failure because it is linked to our greatest learning experiences?

Big Leaper Nicky first hired me because she felt she was 'failing'. At 30, she felt washed up. All her friends were successful and working in great careers, and she had just been made redundant for the third time as a management consultant. 'It's official,' she wailed. 'I'm a failure.' What if there was no such thing as failure and this was the best learning experience of her life? I asked her, 'What are you learning?' 'That I've been in the wrong bloody job for ten years!' she snapped back. So what is the right job?

That question started Nicky off on a path that helped her to identify that she hated working for other people, that she wasn't in the least bit inspired or interested by management consultancy, and that, in fact, she wanted to start her own fashion business. Three years on, Nicky had her own fashion company and TV show.

She says now, 'Without "failing" in corporate life, I would never have discovered my dream and wouldn't be here now. Failing was the best thing I've ever done. It was my wake-up call to life.'

Imagine if every failure was a wake-up call to life? How would this thinking serve you? What if failure was seen as a profoundly positive experience? If it allowed us to re-evaluate our life and our path, and ask ourselves the questions that we probably choose to ignore in less

turbulent times: What do we really want? What are
we good at? What are we truly interested in?

Let's admit that the initial feeling of failing doesn't feel
good. We're disappointed that things didn't work out as we
had hoped, and it can be annoying – but aren't all wake-up
calls? When I'm woken from a deep sleep, I certainly feel
grumpy and irritated. But at least we're alive, breathing
and 'awake'. We're not living a life of quiet desperation,
plodding along on the same old non-challenging path for
years because we're scared of doing something different.

Without that wake-up call, we live with an enemy that is
far greater than failure. It's fear of failure than can truly
do us in. What has your fear of failure stopped you from
doing? From finding the love your life? From creating a
global company? From writing a bestseller? Maybe we
were saved from feeling foolish, but at what cost?

Our fear of failure holds us back, stopping us from trying
and from truly living. Maybe we could have been a
contender, but in the end we were too scared.

In the 1950s in America, one of the best ways struggling
new talent could get a start on the road to fame was to
appear on a nationally televised programme called 'The
Original Amateur Hour'. A singer from Tennessee tried
out for the show, but failed the audition. Imagine if that
singer had defined himself a failure: weak, deficient,
unsuccessful, not good enough (the definition of 'failed' in
the Oxford English Dictionary). The world would never
have known Elvis Presley.

Whether it's Elvis, Margaret Mitchell with 38 rejections
from publishers for *Gone with the Wind*, or Thomas
Edison's many failed experiments before he invented
the lightbulb, what would have happened if they had

been so afraid of making a fool of themselves and of disappointment that they gave up?

How do we make the magical shift from, 'I'm a failure, I'm doomed, I'll never amount to anything,' to 'There's no such thing as failure, just learning experiences'? If you believe that you're not good enough, failure is absolutely invaluable evidence to prove it. In fact, we may constantly, albeit subconsciously, set ourselves up to fail. If this resonates with you, it may be useful to go back and reread Big Leap Step 4. Remember, beliefs are simply a filter through which we see the world and evaluate our experiences to make sure they back up our essential beliefs about ourselves and life.

Our way to a new, magical way of thinking, of 'learning' rather than 'failing', must be built on a foundation of self-belief. Belief that if something does not turn out as we hoped, it doesn't mean that there's something wrong with us. It's about being able to let go of the idea of perfection, of 'getting it right first time', of having a bar of a certain height that we have to jump over to prove ourselves. What if you just knew your worth, no matter what the result of what you were trying to achieve? If our self-belief and self-esteem is wrapped up in what we 'do', then it is easy to see why failure is so painful.

 Jules Ritter, Big Leaping from mother and housewife to writer and journalist

You have to take risks on this journey. You've got to knock on doors and keep on knocking. You have to be willing to be rejected and to fail, but know that you'll be okay no matter what happens. Once I flew all the way to London to meet with a prominent editor only for them to call me in my hotel room and cancel the same morning.

The important thing is to know that no matter what happens, your essence won't be affected. It's to live that old coaching question – what would you do if you knew you couldn't fail? I would rather live my life failing every day on the journey to fulfilment rather than live a life of quiet desperation in a beautiful house. My belief is, 'Leap and the net will appear.' It does and it has. But every time you leap, it takes a lot of courage.

Exercise: WHAT ARE YOU LEARNING?

When you hear the whispers of the fear of failure, answer the following questions in your journal.

- How are things not turning out as you hoped?
- What would happen if you let go of the outcome?
- How could these results be a call to action?
- What Big Leap in thinking do you need to take?
- If you were to look back at this 'crisis' 10 years from now, what do you think you will have learned from it?
- If this were to be the moment when you completely reinvented your idea/business/thinking, what three actions would you take or not take?

Marc Lockley, Big Leaping from Head of Agency Sales to business owner, author and online columnist

I often have real dark moments of self-doubt. When the phone doesn't ring, or I feel isolated, I can get myself really strung out. How do I deal with it? I give myself a firm talking-to. The world isn't at an end. No one is terminally ill. I'm not on the streets. I allow myself five minutes to wallow in worry. Then I get my 'positive thinking' book out and write at least 10 things that are really good right now. It's the best tool I've found, because all you have to do is look back through the pages and you realize how good you have it in your life.

Sometimes it's useful to take some 'under the duvet' time, as I call it. Time when we stop pushing, stop checking our emails to discover if anyone has replied, and simply take time out and let life get on with it. It goes against every notion we have in Western society, but sometimes 'giving in', surrendering, is exactly what we need to do. When we push really hard and get overly intent on a particular outcome, we don't realize that life has other plans. We're so close to the process that we can't see the grand scheme. Our Inner Pessimist gets more and more panicked by the lack of results, giving him more ammunition to throw at us. So when he finally throws the 'failure' grenade into our laps, we explode.

Sometimes we need an explosion – to explode our beliefs, our expectations and our plans. In the aftermath, we're so exhausted and shocked that we finally find some peace and can hear what our Inner Coach has been telling us all along. Usually she'll tell us that there's no such thing as failure and ask if we had thought of trying to do things another way. Our journey begins afresh once again.

 Keris Stainton, Big Leaping from an administration job to a full-time novelist

After about a year of freelancing, I had to sign up with a temp agency. Even though I was getting work, cash flow was erratic. So I found myself back in a windowless office, doing exactly the thing I'd hated doing for so many years. I was scared I'd just get sucked back into it all again, but thankfully that didn't happen.

My Inner Pessimist's refrain of 'What makes you think you're a writer? This is where you belong!' had been replaced by my Inner Coach's: 'What are you doing here? You know you're a writer.' I only temped for two days.

Baby step 3:
Heartbreak

Sometimes our Big Low has nothing to do with money or work; our 'failure' involves loss or heartbreak. In the Victorian era, people who lost a loved one wore black for a year to mourn and honour them. Today we hardly pause for breath after a funeral, divorce or heartbreak.

Life can throw us some tough shots. We lose people we love, your husband sleeps with someone else, your wife stops loving you, you watch your mother die after seeing her flesh fade from her bones, you miscarry, again …

Pain. It's there. Sometimes you just can't avoid it. We've all got our story. We've all got our pain. But the important question is: what do we do with it? Smile a brittle smile and look on the bright side of life? Or do we become defined by it? Orphan, widower, infertile, depressed, unemployed. Do we bury it, trying to just 'get over it'? I suggest we do none of the above, but simply go through it. Feel it and get to the other side. This is the act of transformation. This is the ultimate act of courage. You have to be the hero in your own story.

I don't know how you feel. But I do know that we all have our own tragedies, our own stories, our own shame. I believe the longer we carry that pain around with us, the heavier it gets. Then we have to use all sorts of strategies to hide from and avoid it, be it drinking a vat of wine or working a 70-hour week.

The way out? To feel it. You're going to feel low and sad and bad. There's nothing wrong with that. Don't cover it over. This step might hurt. But I would suggest there is more suffering in hiding from pain. When we do this, we live our lives in the shadows. By avoiding the thing we're afraid of, we live half-lives.

We need to be willing to walk through the doorway. Be sad, be angry: feel it. Stop running away from yourself. This is not about being nice or positive. This is about being raw and honest with yourself. No more covering up. It's time to be brave. To roar, to burn, to step into the fire. No more hiding, no more, 'Have a nice day.' Have a terrible day, go into hibernation, wail, rasp and be real. Let it out. Get help – you don't have to do it alone. Find someone, a professional or a friend, who will listen to you through this healing process, so that you don't have to hold it together or hold it in.

Ready to leap

Exercise: HEALING HEARTBREAK

Imagine how you could create a ceremony or some kind of physical way to honour your loss and heartbreak: for example, making a photo album, visiting a grave, or creating a bonfire to burn old possessions. How would you celebrate the passing of someone or something?

I'm a great fan of Chinese 'wish' lanterns that you light and then release into the sky. I use them to signify that I'm letting go of someone or something in my life. I stand in the garden, light my lantern, and then usually cry as I wave it off into the sky. God knows what the neighbours think but it works for me. What would work for you?

Baby step 4:
Surrender!

Often the Big Low depresses us because we have been
focusing on a certain outcome – a business deal, a
marriage proposal, a baby, a job, a cheque in the post, a
loved one healed. When we don't get what we thought
we wanted, our faith and hope is destroyed. There is no
dream. We lost the battle, we lost it all.

On every journey worth taking or story worth telling, this
step is when the hero discovers a new solution, sees
something in a new way and understands that 'winning'
what they thought they wanted isn't important any more
as they learn something key about life or themselves.

I admit, it's hard to see this outcome when you're
wallowing in fear or pain. If anyone tries to be positive
at this point, you want to tell them to go away in a not
so very polite way. When you're deep in your dark place,
it is virtually impossible to think (or act) positively.
There's only one place left to sink. Sink into a place
of surrender.

I've heard many gurus speak on the concept of surrender
– surrendering to the gods, the universe, the flow of life.
Call me a control freak, but I've not always been that
good at it. I'd rather weep and wail and rail. Not that it
makes me feel any better or gets me better results.
However, recently I discovered a brilliant technique
developed by consciousness teacher Asara Lovejoy. The
main goal of her method is to manifest wealth in your
life, but I have found the process just as effective for
surrendering your pain and getting in a more powerfully
creative (versus victimized) place using a six-step process
she calls 'The One Command'.

This is a visualization technique that slows the brainwaves to the theta state – that relaxed, daydreaming, hypnotic state we normally experience just before we fall asleep and just after we wake up. Our brainwaves are measured as micro-electrical charges per second. The brainwave we are most familiar with is beta – 13–30 cycles per second, known as our waking, or conscious mind. The alpha state, measured at 7–13 cycles per second is known as our meditative or contemplative mind. Theta is 4–7 cycles per second and is what Lovejoy calls 'the source mind'. She says:

In theta, you reconnect to your natural, creative intelligence, and disengage from the fearful, limited world view of what is possible. You develop a natural sense of security and trust in the world. The thoughts you have in theta are more powerful than your ordinary thoughts, and they bring about changes in your life quickly and easily.

Ready to leap

Exercise: THE ONE COMMAND

Try out Lovejoy's six-step process. Ask a friend to help you if you can. First, write the names of each of the six steps below on a separate piece of paper.

1. Ground
2. Align
3. Go to theta
4. Command
5. Expand
6. Receive with gratitude

Place the six pieces of paper in a horizontal line on the floor. You are going to stand on each piece of paper and get your friend to read the steps out to you. Stay on each step until you complete your visualization, taking as much time as you need, and then move sideways to the next step.

Before you step on 'Ground', think of something you want in your life, be it inner peace, better health or a relationship. Now close your eyes and keep them closed throughout the process. Have your friend read the directions below slowly at each step as they guide you through the process. Stay at each step until you know you are ready to continue.

Step 1: Ground
Feel the weight of your body settling onto the paper beneath your feet. Now imagine roots coming out from the bottom of your feet and send them down, deep into the earth. Connect with the 'magnetic power' of the earth, the basis and foundation of all our support. Imagine you are wrapping your roots around gold, diamonds and rubies in the centre of the earth. Feel the power of that energy grounding and balancing you. Stay here until you feel your body shift into a well-grounded state.

Step 2: Align
When you are ready, move sideways to the second step (let your friend guide you if necessary by holding on to your waist), and stand on 'Align'. Imagine all that power of the earth's energy coming into your body and into your heart. Now take a deep breath, and as you exhale, imagine that the energy is expanding in all directions around you. The breath of your heart is expanding above, below and all around you. As you exhale, the breath is aligning you with a feeling of unconditional love.

Step 3: Go to theta

Now move sideways to the third step 'Go to theta'. Imagine a golden beam of light, a field of energy flowing into you from the far-distant reaches of the galaxies, flowing down through you and out below you, deep into the earth. Imagine moving your consciousness up this beam of light, out of the top of your head, above your head, out to the outer edges of the planet, on through the solar system, beyond the galaxy, until you push through the black void of space and into the white light of 'source'. Feel how this feels and amplify that feeling.

Step 4: Command

While thinking of what you want to create more of in your life, mentally and silently command, 'I don't know how … [fill in the blank: e.g. to let go of my negative thinking; to let go of my addictions; to forgive; to create a loving relationship; to achieve wellness; to create abundance in my life.] I only know that I do now, and I am fulfilled!' Take your time to allow this declaration to resonate in your body before you take the next step.

(Note: I have found this command to be incredibly powerful. My whole conscious mind switches off and relaxes when I say the words 'I don't know how'. This technique allows me to surrender and stop trying to control consciously, leaving my 'source mind' – my creative, imaginative mind – to come up with the answers. Not that it comes up with answers at this point. I just choose to have faith (which is the 'I only know that I do now' part) that a solution to any challenge I'm struggling with will present itself. I have discovered that within hours or days, my creative mind is usually inspired with some solutions and answers. Or I just feel differently about the issue and my focus shifts. What you focus on expands.)

Step 5: Expand

While you are still in theta, imagine what you desire in a bigger way, a greater capacity, an expanded version that serves more good than your original idea. For example, if you want to feel more peaceful, imagine what impact that might have on the people around you, the life you might create differently if you lived from this perspective. Think really big! Go wild, and watch as new, expanded, bigger ideas arrive. Stay in the process until your vision is as big as it will go. Now move on to Step 6.

Step 6: Receive with gratitude

Imagine that your 'request' has been granted. State in your mind clearly, 'Thank you! It is so!' Experience a sense of gratitude and fulfilment. Remember, your mind does not know the difference between real and imagined. While in a state of gratitude, imagine moving your consciousness back. Feel the golden beam of light coming gently back into your physical body, and imagine the particles of your vision floating down from the source into your body, then into the cells of your body and into your DNA itself. Imagine unwinding, unwinding, unwinding all the old limiting ideas and rewinding, rewinding, rewinding a new holographic image of your vision. Imagine your new life replicating itself in every DNA strand in every organ of your body, in every hair follicle of your body, and in every particle of emotion in your thinking. Feel it, accept it and give thanks. Take a deep breath and imagine sending your energy back down into the earth to 'ground' yourself. Stretch and flex and take all the time you need to come, once again, fully awake in the room. Open your eyes.

Take time to share anything you've discovered while doing this process with your friend.

Lovejoy recommends repeating this process twice the first time you do it. Then practise every day until it becomes so natural that you can go through the six steps mentally, instantly, any time that you wish to change or let go of old behaviours or thinking patterns. Practise until this becomes an unconscious internal process.

That's all for Big Leap Step 6. It is likely to be exhausting, so my final suggestion is just to go to bed. Try not to drink alcohol or numb yourself with dubious substances. Just go to bed early and sleep. Treat yourself like a child – gently, lovingly. You'll need your strength for the morning. This dark night of the soul will pass, I promise.

Your Inner Pessimist is probably saying right now ...

'Go to sleep? What are you talking about? There is far too much to worry about to sleep. What are you going to do? OH MY GOD! WHAT ARE YOU GOING TO DO? This is just terrible. I always knew this was going to happen if you listened to her. I told you so.'

What you need to be doing right now ...

Tune in to your Inner Coach. Write down in your journal what she has to say about all this.

The Big Leap

'Tap your heels together.'

'Our deepest fear is not that we are inadequate. Our deepest fear is that we are powerful beyond measure. It is our light, not our darkness that most frightens us. We ask ourselves, Who am I to be brilliant, gorgeous, talented, fabulous? Actually, who are you not to be?'

– MARIANNE WILLIAMSON,
AUTHOR OF
A RETURN TO LOVE (1952–)

Big Leap Step 7:   **THE BABY STEPS**

1. Take one baby step, then another …
2. The gloop zone
3. Meet the saboteurs
4. Mind the gap!
5. 450 baby steps – a 90-day plan
6. The Big Leap – your homework

You've finally made it to the last step of the journey. The dawn has broken on a new era, a new way of life has begun. Feel proud of yourself for coming so far – it's one hell of a journey. The most exciting part is just about to begin. You've done all the work beneath the surface, you've started to change, and you feel different to the way you used to. This is the bit when, like Dorothy, you realize you have everything you need to go back 'home'. You hold all the resources to create what you want in your life. Now it's time to go out into the world and start making the changes that will make your dreams come true. Get ready! It's time for action! This is your grand finale. Time to step up and take centre stage.

What you're probably thinking at Big Leap Step 7

- I can do this!
- Just watch me, everyone!
- I'm so excited!
- I'm a bit nervous, but you know what? I think I can do this.
- This is it!
- Watch out world, here I come.

What you're probably doing at Big Leap Step 7

- Putting new goals in your diary.
- Telling everyone to expect 'a few changes around here'.
- Throwing your cigarette packet out of the window/ buying an exercise bike/signing up to recruitment agencies/resigning from your job.
- Throwing a party to signify your new life.
- Uncluttering your wardrobe/office/living room in preparation for your new life.
- Having your hair cut, buying new clothes.

You're almost there. This is the really exciting step where you get to take lots of action, make your dreams real and make it all happen. We've still got some obstacles to leap over so stick close. Let's do it.

Baby step 1:
Take one baby step, then another ...

You've finally got to Big Leap Step 7. Now it's time to stop thinking and talking about it and start making it happen. We've been working on the 'being' part, now you're required to do something – and differently to how you've done it before. Keep in mind the old adage that the definition of madness is doing the same thing, but expecting different results.

So are you ready? Are your pencils sharpened, your shoes shiny, your new diary opened to a crisp new page? Are you ready to manifest the physical reality that has been created by your leap in thinking? This is the only time I'm going to say this, but on this occasion, I don't want you to take a leap. I want you to take a baby step.

When we create exciting visions of our future, it can feel overwhelming and unrealistic at first, and this is a danger point. We can simply dismiss the idea and go back to our comfort zones, hearing the whispers of our Inner Coach calling, but then simply turning up the TV so we can't hear her.

The first step in acting on your vision is the scariest, but it's the most significant. It shows you are willing to leave your comfort zone. But taking action can often be overwhelming. You don't know where to start. You look up at the mountain, and the path to the top looks too far and too long. Suddenly you feel as if you'll never get there.

That's why it's so important to take it one day at a time. Cut everything down into baby steps and keep going forwards. You'll set yourself up to succeed if you stop looking to the top of the mountain and just look down at the next step you're going to take. Repeat after me, 'I will achieve my goal with baby steps.'

By breaking the Big Leap down into baby steps, we creep out of our comfort zone without our fear sirens screaming, 'You're not good enough. You're going to fail.' I know we have talked about this journey being based on our golden glow moments, but fear can still sabotage us big-style in the early days. We need to take it slowly, making the steps small and manageable. The Big Leap support team have suggested three first baby steps that they found to be helpful.

First step: Get help

It's amazing who you already know that can make a difference to your success. Or if you don't, you'll probably know someone who knows someone who can help. You'll be surprised how much people actually like to help and share their knowledge. We all know how special and wanted it can make us feel if someone approaches us as an 'expert'. I always feel incredibly flattered when someone wants to pick my brains. So who do you know that can help you?

Make a list of potential mentors, enthusiastic friends, friends of parents, and old bosses who can help you work towards your goal, and then create a group email to send to everyone and ask for help. Be specific: state exactly what your goal is and give concrete examples of what it is that you need – e.g. does anyone's company do so and so? Can I pick your brains about such and such an idea? Does anyone know anyone in New York that I can stay with?

Second step: Get support

Form a Big Leap support group of your own. Get your
two best and most positive friends on board. Tell them
your plans and ask them to be there for you and to tell
you, 'You can do it,' 'You're amazing,' 'Of course, you can
run for president!' whenever you're having a crisis of
confidence. It is so important to create a support team of
friends or colleagues – a 'power team' – who can hold
your hand when you feel tired and emotional and who
will applaud your triumphs. Make sure you avoid
negative pessimists like the plague.

Recently, on one of my latest Big Leap odysseys, I found
myself in the Big Low and I made the big mistake of
phoning two people who not only had no support to offer,
but also told me that I needed to get a grip, give up and
accept defeat. When we are on the Big Leap journey, we
are incredibly vulnerable and need support. When we
think we cannot go on, a friend or colleague needs to
smile and say, 'Come on, sunshine, there's no going back.
Let's keep on going.'

 **Nicky Hambleton-Jones, Big Leaping from management
consultant to celebrity fashion stylist**

*People think you need contacts to start a business or be successful
– it's that 'It's who you know, not what you know' line. That's
rubbish. I didn't know a single soul in fashion, but still managed
to create a business in the fashion industry.*

*It's not contacts that you need, it's your support team – your
coach, your friends, those people who believe in you 110
percent. They are the ones who will tell you to keep the faith in
your darkest hour, and who'll push you to keep going when you
doubt yourself.*

Third step: Find your tribe

It can be very difficult to create the life you want if you are surrounded by people who think you're slightly odd for even trying. They can make you feel like you're either insane or headed for a mighty fall. Instead you need to surround yourself with like-minded people, people who are also creating their dreams. Seek them out: for support, for laughs and for inspiration.

On my Big Leap journey, I have often been really inspired by others – sometimes just at the right time. My business was turned around by going to a presentation and hearing Simon Woodroffe (the business entrepreneur and creator of Yo!Sushi) challenging everyone in the audience to do tomorrow what we had been putting off for months. The day after his talk, I sent an email that got me a column in the national press. I may never have sent that email if I hadn't been with people who had been there themselves (and got the T-shirt).

Jules Ritter, Big Leaping from mother and housewife to writer and journalist

Your net worth is your network. When I started to pitch, I got my first commission from a travel magazine and I was so excited. I sent in the article I wrote and then they rejected it. I was devastated.

My best friend sat with me in the garden and said, 'Come on, it's just one setback. What? You're going to give up now?' 'No, I'm not,' I thought. But without that support and help, it would have been much harder.

Baby step 2:
The gloop zone

Go on, then. What are you waiting for? You've written your lists of baby steps, your friends are screaming support from the sidelines, and you've joined a networking group. Now what? What do you mean 'Nothing'?

Welcome to the gloop zone. This is that terrifying void of non-action when something gets in the way of taking the first step: the baby's up all night; the boss decided to call an early morning meeting; your partner is having a crisis and needs your help; and all of a sudden your good intentions fly out the window.

A day passes when you've done nothing to build evidence to prove that your new life is possible, and then another, and you sink further and further into the gloop. You feel your passionate fervour ebbing away until you find yourself at the end of the week in the same chair, watching the same TV programme, thinking 'Noooooooooooooooo!'

The Inner Pessimist loves the gloop zone. 'Ah, you see, I told you that you couldn't do it.' It feeds off your inertia. 'Well, you've tried. Never mind. It's time you came back to reality.' The gloop zone is where I usually turn into a cynic. It's where I blame the process: 'That book? Oh, yeah, I read it, too, but it just doesn't work.' It is where my best intentions are knobbled. It's the place where I threw my cigarette packet out of the window, bought an exercise bike and signed up to a yoga class – and then did nothing. The gloop zone is the place where I've read self-help books while fishing dog-ends of cigarettes out of the bin to smoke, watched dust gathering on the exercise bike, and been so hungover that I'd have to stop reading and lie down, promising that my new regime would start tomorrow.

10 ways you'll know that you're in the gloop zone

1. You say things like, 'I'll start tomorrow.'
2. You find yourself avoiding looking in your diary.
3. If your friends or family mention that they thought you were doing that new thing, you get angry, saying, 'Don't give me a hard time!'
4. You find yourself doing displacement activities like shopping/drinking in the pub/watching TV.
5. You find yourself getting involved in other people's dramas.
6. You feel lethargic.
7. Your home either becomes a tip as you sit around and pick your toenails, or it becomes a palace as you clean every surface for the fifth time: 'I'll just get sorted out before I start.'
8. You drink 14 cups of tea a day.
9. You eat non-stop.
10. You find yourself volunteering for other people's errands. 'I'll pick up your dry cleaning for you!'

In some ways, being in the gloop zone is even worse than being in denial in Big Leap Step 1 because now it's conscious. You know why you've been unhappy, you know what little scams you've been running, and you still find yourself sitting in the same chair. The gloop zone becomes a pit of despair and self-loathing as your Inner Pessimist sits beside you, gloating and patronizing you. 'It's okay, dear, you've done ever so well, but a fulfilled life? Not for you, really, is it?'

How long we stay in the gloop zone is usually in direct relation to how scared we are about making our Big Leap. Staying there is just another way to keep ourselves safe. At this point we have to be very, very kind to ourselves. You've probably been here a million times before, and how has beating yourself up about it ever helped? Your Inner Pessimist is so terrified right now that he'd sell your grandma to keep you where you are. Sometimes the best thing to do is to crawl under the duvet and simply acknowledge that you're in the gloop zone.

Ready to leap

Exercise: GET OUT OF THE GLOOP ZONE

When you're ready, answer the following questions in your journal.

- What are you scared might happen if you take a baby step?
- What's the absolute worst-case scenario?
- How would you handle that?
- What is the tiniest baby step you can make today?
- How could you make it tinier?
- What can you commit to doing when you get out of bed?

Baby step 3:
Meet the saboteurs

Once you start taking your baby steps out of the gloop, you'll be slowly creeping your way out of your comfort zone. Or maybe you're storming your way out: you've written your resignation letter, you've got your meetings planned, you're all set to head off to a sunnier climate to look at some properties, or you're about to go on a first date. Your Inner Pessimist seems fairly quiet, but then you start to notice some other weird noises and behaviours.

It's time to meet the saboteurs, the second cousins of the Inner Pessimist. Your saboteurs tend to gang together on the street corners of your inner fears. Effectively, they gather around you and look threatening, stopping you from moving forward. They are very familiar, old behaviours that you have in place, which slow you down or sabotage your success. Just as with the Inner Pessimist, it's no good doing battle with them. You created them unconsciously because you were terrified – of success, of failure, of not being good enough, whatever it was. So don't try to ignore them or bully them into submission; it won't work. You have to be gentle with yourself and them. Bring them into the light of awareness and discover the next layer of fear that is stopping you from moving forward.

Procrastination is my chief saboteur. In fact, I'd say that procrastination is one of my greatest skills. I've become such a master at procrastination and it has become so subtle that I can fool myself into thinking that I'm not procrastinating at all, but in the middle of the 'creative process' or 'doing research' or 'getting in touch with my feelings', when in fact, I'm out shopping and drinking coffee with my best friend.

I'm good at creating the big vision, talking-the-talk, describing how my life will look in five years, getting everyone excited and busting my scams. This can go on for days, months and sometimes even years. I dream, I plan, I visualize – but do nothing. My best friend always raises an eyebrow when I get out my coloured pens and draw circles around ideas and write up a little schedule of when I'm going to get it done (always starting tomorrow, of course).

Tomorrow is a lovely place to park your dreams because if you plan your procrastination well, tomorrow never comes. 'Tomorrow' you don't have to be disappointed when someone you're expecting doesn't turn up, devastated when the answer is 'no', frustrated when the banks laugh at your business plan, humiliated when you fail so spectacularly that even your biggest fans start to doubt you.

Procrastination allows you to live in I-could've-been-a-contender land, which sometimes feels a lot more pleasant than the imagined sound of mocking laughter. I know exactly why I procrastinate, and sometimes I let myself settle there comfortably for a day or two while I gather my courage and prepare to throw myself out of my comfort zone again.

As human beings, we're not stupid. Our saboteurs are there to protect us, to try to keep us safe. However, to live the life you really want, you have to venture out of your comfort zone and make the Big Leap. Part of that leap means bringing your saboteurs into awareness. I have detailed the seven main saboteurs below. Once you have read them all, complete the exercise and write your sabotaging symptoms on a big sheet of paper so no matter how wily you may be, you will never be able to convince yourself that shopping and drinking white wine with your best friend is research.

Saboteur number 1: the Procrastinator

Style:
Shifty

Most likely to say:
'I'll just clean the house from top to bottom before I start.'

You know you're sabotaging when:
- You spend every day rewriting your vision.
- You spend all your time telling everyone what your new life will look like, but do nothing different.

- Your house/office/desk is always scrupulously tidy. Once everything is tidy, you can start working on the baby steps tomorrow.
- You decide to start taking action once you stop smoking/are in a better position/get married/move house/lose weight.
- You don't make the phone call because everyone's away for the holidays/for the summer/the kids are off school.
- You don't make the call because the person you want to contact might be on their mobile/in a meeting.
- You spend the whole day on the Internet 'researching'. Once you have a bit more information, you'll make the call.

Why do you do it?
It's easier to put off living your dreams than to face possible disappointments, heartbreaks and failure. By procrastinating, you live the fantasy, but you are not actually moving forward.

Saboteur number 2: the Overpromiser

Style:
Effusive, big gestures, large sums bandied about

Most likely to say:
'By this time next year, we'll be millionaires.'

You know you're sabotaging when:
- You talk and your friends' eyes glaze over.
- You talk and the bank manager says, 'Er, are we both looking at the same account?'
- You consistently set goals that you never reach.
- Your credit card is declined – often.
- Even you don't believe your hype.

- You spend more time shopping for the accessories for your new lifestyle than getting on with doing what needs to be done to get there.

Why do you do it?
By living in a 'bigged up world', you don't have to face the nitty-gritty reality of putting in the hours and confronting your fears.

Saboteur number 3: the Flake

Style:
Flaky

Most likely to say:
'Oops, I left the baby on the bus!'

You know you're sabotaging when:
- You show up late to important meetings.
- You miss trains.
- You 'don't hear' the alarm.
- You lose the keys to the car.
- You lock yourself out of the car/the house/the office.
- You can't find important business cards/files.

Why do you do it?
Playing flaky means you don't have to take responsibility if your plans don't come to fruition. You can blame failure on everyone and everything else – the late train or the broken alarm.

Saboteur number 4: the Wild Child

Style:
Hunched

Most likely to say:
'I don't give a s**t what you think.'

You know you're sabotaging when:
- You're rude to important people.
- You have too much to drink and behave inappropriately at a business social occasion.
- You drink too much the night before a big day.
- You turn up to important meetings in inappropriate clothes.
- You turn up to important meetings late, smelling of alcohol and smoke.

Why do you do it?
You're terrified that someone will attack you or tell you your idea can't work, so you hunch into a defensive stance and hope that they'll be too scared to try.

Saboteur number 5: the Perfectionist

Style:
Scary, bossy and controlling

Most likely to say:
'Rewrite it.'

You know you're sabotaging when:
- You rewrite something seven times and it's still not right.
- You refuse to send it out until it's perfect.
- You fixate on one route and one route only and insist that this is the only way.

- You tell everyone how to do his or her job.
- You tell everyone that they're wrong and you're right.
- Your voice gets more and more clipped.
- You criticize others for not getting small details right.

Why do you do it?

Terror of moving forward keeps you seeking perfection. If it's not perfect, you know it won't work. So why risk rejection and failure just yet?

Saboteur number 6: the Beach Bum

Style:

Horizontal

Most likely to say:

'Don't get your knickers in a twist. I'm doing it in my own time.'

You know you're sabotaging when:

- You light 'just one more' cigarette/have 'just one more' beer.
- You smile charmingly and shrug when anyone asks you a specific question about your plans.
- You sit around with other people that have beach bum behaviour and 'just chill'.
- You buy a skateboard to help you get creative.

Why do you do it?

You're terrified of committing to something. Deep down, you don't think you have the resources to make it happen, so you 'chill' instead.

Saboteur number 7: the Feeler

Style:
Anxious

Most likely to say:
'Let's talk about how I'm feeling.'

You know you're sabotaging when:
- You fantasize about how your life will be when you're 'discovered', but do nothing.
- You write your Oscar speech rather than your CV.
- You want everything to be 'beautiful', but because everything isn't, you do nothing.
- You talk endlessly about your feelings to your friends.
- You enviously obsess about what other people have or are doing with their lives.
- You live in a fantasy land in the future, resisting anything that feels 'ordinary'.

Why do you do it?
You are terrified that you can't create the life you want, fearing that the reality will never live up to the fantasy.

Exercise: IDENTIFY YOUR SABOTEURS

Ready to leap

Answer the following questions in your journal.

- What are your usual saboteurs?
- What is your particular sabotage style?
- What do you usually say when in sabotage mode?
- Describe in great detail the series of events (actions you take or don't take) when you're sabotaging yourself.
- What are your top three sabotaging symptoms? (Shopping? Skateboarding? Discussing feelings?)

Ann Norton, Big Leaping from Melbourne, Australia to London, England

I was born in London and had always loved it, but ended up moving and living in Australia with my husband Ken. I stayed there when he died in 1997. However, I always had a longing to move back to London. As much as I liked Australia, London was always my spiritual and cultural home.

My daughter Lucy, 23, had moved out, so I was once again independent and free to travel wherever I wanted. I wanted to be in London, but even when I allowed myself to daydream, my Inner Pessimist said, 'I can't afford to do it. How will I support myself? How will I survive? I'm too old to move at 57.' Every time I thought of making the move, I would just procrastinate and procrastinate. For me, the greatest two decisions I made were hiring a British coach who was a link to my new world, and buying a plane ticket. I then had to get on with it. It's about making the decision and then committing to it. You have to beat those inner saboteurs by taking action.

The saboteur antidote

So what's the answer? Awareness is the key: awareness and baby steps. Once we know how we sabotage ourselves and can catch it in the process, we're halfway there. We can then acknowledge that we're scared, but as self-help author Susan Jeffers says, 'Feel the fear and do it anyway.' Make it as painless and not scary as possible by taking a baby step. As soon as you take a small step towards your goal, the fear recedes, with the result that you are able to move forward again. I call it 'exercising the courage muscle'. The more you exercise this muscle, the stronger it gets. Before you know it, you're taking massive leaps, with no saboteurs lurking on the horizon.

Saboteur antidote

- Awareness + Baby Step = Little Leap
- Little Leap + Little Leap + Little Leap
  (to strengthen courage muscles) = Big Leap

I know 'Just do it' is a cliché but right now it's about taking action and building momentum. Write down ten tiny baby steps and just do it in the next ten minutes. Move. Create. Pick up the phone. Book an appointment. Just do it.

Nicky Hambleton-Jones, Big Leaping from management consultant to celebrity fashion stylist

I had my business idea, had the business plan, had been on the styling course and I think I could have spent a year procrastinating designing logos, letterheads and websites before getting my first client. But my coach bullied me (she calls it 'motivation'!) into styling my first-ever client and taking her out on a shopping trip. I nearly died of nerves – but I did it. The results were fantastic. My client loved it and felt completely transformed. A week later, she flew off on a holiday and met the love of her life. It really boosted my confidence.

I think it's a common mistake to make when you start your new business. You spend ages concentrating on the details rather than on the brass tacks. If I didn't have any clients, I wouldn't have a business. That first client will always be terrifying, but whatever you have to do to get through the fear – just do it.

Baby step 4:
Mind the gap!

Even when you've made your way out of the gloop and found your saboteur antidote, I'm afraid to say there may still be times when you feel as if you're going insane. You have the vision in place, your business cards are printed, you have big plans afoot for global domination, but you're in debt and still working out of your back bedroom or in a full-time job you don't like. You have created the vision board of your ideal man, joined several dating websites, but have not been on one date. You have bought a new laptop, been on five creative-writing courses, but still haven't completed a page of your novel yet.

The gap between how you envision your new life and the reality of how it is right now can sometimes seem too ludicrously wide. You wonder whether you're simply a fantasist who makes things up so they feel better. Your Inner Pessimist sniggers knowingly as you open a bank statement and feel your heart drop, or open your 'novel' and see merely one sentence gracing a very white page.

How do you survive these moments when your Inner Pessimist urges you to turn back, reassuring you that despite a good effort, it's time to go back to reality? How do you keep going when all the signs tell you to 'be realistic'?

At points like this in the journey, it's useful to check in with yourself. If the journey is becoming too much of a struggle, it's usually because your belief is wavering and an emotional need is not being met. To get back on track, go back to the Big Leap basics.

Exercise: BIG LEAP CHECKLIST

Ready to leap **?**

Answer the following questions in your journal.

1. Needy?
What emotional need is not being met right now?
What do I need that I'm not getting? How can I get that need met?

2. Tuned in to the wrong station?
Who am I listening to, my Inner Pessimist or my Inner Coach?
Meditate for 15 minutes and then write down what your Inner Coach has to say.

3. Bingo moment?
Does my vision excite me and make me feel inspired and uplifted, even if I don't know how on earth I'm going to create it?

4. Belief?
What assumptions am I making that are blocking me?
What do I need to believe about myself and life to enable me to make the next step?

5. Scams?
What old behaviours are showing up that might be slowing me down?
What is at the root of these scams?

6. Saboteurs?
How am I sabotaging myself?
What tiny baby step can I take in the next 10 minutes?

Baby step 5:
450 baby steps –
a 90-day plan

Once you've got your energy flowing again, I want you to keep moving. I don't want you to stop. Create a 90-day plan by taking five baby steps a day and 25 baby steps a week. Create a special notebook and write a list of five baby steps for every day of the first week (but not for the whole 90 days, as things tend to change and speed up as the month goes on). Your baby steps can be small, such as a phone call to a business development agency or a call to book a meeting with a dating agency or adoption agency. The main objective is to plant your seeds. Every baby step that you take is another seed planted.

Set yourself up to succeed by celebrating at the end of every week. Ring your support group and get them to cheer loudly. Don't wait until you've climbed your mountain before you throw the party; celebrate every molehill you leap over. It will help give you momentum. At the end of 30 days, reflect, congratulate yourself, and then plan the next 30 days. What has worked? What hasn't worked? Use the foundation and confidence you have built over the last 30 days to create a springboard for the next seed-planting mission.

Remember: if you keep on doing what you've always done, you'll keep on getting what you've always got. The main focus is to keep taking action and to keep planting your seeds. They can take a while to grow, but by the end of your 90-day programme, you might see the first few shoots of your new life. It is incredible how fast a garden can grow if the ground is fertile. You've done all the hard work, so there is no reason why your garden should not grow at an inspiring rate.

Anne Thorn, Big Leaping from lonely singledom to a vibrant social life

I was a 50-year-old single woman. If you believed the media, I was an 'invisible' woman. Forget it, the world seemed to say – you're past it. But I'm not, I'm 50 years young, as I always say. I don't want to live a boring, unfulfilled life. You have to believe in yourself to make the leap. That doesn't happen without work. You have to take the baby steps. You can sit on your bum all you want and wish for everything to change, but unless you take action, nothing will. There is always a way to make a change, you just have to find it. For me, it started with putting an ad in the paper. From there, I built a website of a community of like-minded people. Now I'm out there, surrounded by friends and dating again. It all started with one baby step.

Baby step 6:
The Big Leap – your homework

It may take a little longer than 90 days. It may take a year, maybe even two or three, but you will reach a point when the momentum means you no longer have to drive it: you finally meet 'the one'; watching the sun come up over Hong Kong's harbour is a regular occurrence rather than an occasional one; you've created your website and the orders are flooding in.

This doesn't mean that you can sit back and put your journal away. I'm afraid I'm going to leave you with some homework. This is an ongoing journey. As we've discussed before, it's not about getting 'there'. You're 'there' already. You're 'there' now. You create your life in this moment, no waiting allowed. Your Big Leap in thinking is just one thought away. That's why it helps to keep your journal up to date and with you at all times. Writing in your journal is an excellent way to coach yourself to keep on making your leaps. It's a great way to keep in touch with your Inner Coach and also a good place for your Inner Pessimist to have a good old rant where you can keep an eye on them.

So don't put your journal away. Let it be your magical wand of transformation. Let it be the safe place where you bring your demons, saboteurs and scams into the light of awareness so they no longer lurk in the dark, destroying your dreams. The more aware we become of the fears that block us, the more we can make true choices about where we want to direct our lives. Let your journal be the place where you reconnect with your Inner Coach, where their voice begins to get strong and clear, where you are able to recognize their wisdom and take actions from a new place of knowing. Let it be the place where you truly celebrate your success – where you learn to cheer yourself on, to be kind to yourself, to give yourself the positive, affirming messages that you may have always longed for, but could never hear over the ranting of your Inner Pessimist.

Let your journal be a book of hope when all the light seems to dim, let it be your inspiration and your manual to guide you to your new life – your own personal guidebook for your new way of working, living and being.

Your Inner Pessimist is probably saying right now ...

'Gawd, she doesn't give up, does she? Glass of wine anyone?'

Your Inner Coach is probably saying right now ...

Smile. Relax. Enjoy.

Suzy's projects

To find out more about Suzy Greaves's projects, visit her websites:

- www.thebigbravelife.com
- For career change: www.thebig-leap.com
- To enjoy the Big Leap journey, log on to Suzy's blog: www.thebigpeace.com

Further reading

Adrienne, Carol, *The Purpose of Your Life*, Piatkus, 1999

Bacci, Ingrid, *The Art of Effortless Living*, Bantam, 2000

Beck, Martha, *Finding Your Own North Star: Claiming the Life You Were Meant to Live*, Piatkus, 2003

Beck, Martha, *The Joy Diet*, Piatkus, 2003

Britten, Rhonda, *Fearless Living,* Mobius, 2002

Chopra, Deepak, *The Way of The Wizard*, Rider, 2000

Coppock, Duncan, *The Self Factor: The Power of Being You: A Coaching Approach*, Findhorn, 2005

Dass, Ram, *Be Here Now*, Crown, 1971

Goddard, Gabriella, *Gulp! The Seven-day Crash Course to Master Fear and Break Through Any Challenge,* Penguin, 2006

Goldberg, Natalie, *Writing Down The Bones*, Shambhala, 2005

Greaves, Suzy, *The Big Peace,* Hay House, 2009

Jeffers, Susan, *Feel the Fear and Do It Anyway*, Rider, 2007

Levine, Stephen, *A Gradual Awakening*, Gateway Books, 2008

Leonard, Thomas J., *The Portable Coach*, Simon Schuster, 1999

Miedaner, Talane, *Coach Yourself to Success*, Contemporary Books, 2001

Orman, Suzy, *The Courage To Be Rich,* Random House, 2002

Roth, Gabrielle, *Sweat Your Prayers*, Newleaf, 1999

Snyder, Blake, *Save the Cat! The Last Book on Screenwriting You'll Ever Need*, Michael Wiese Productions, 2005

Seligman, Martin, *Learned Optimism: How to Change Your Mind and Your Life*, Vintage Books, 2006

Seligman, Martin, *What You Can Change and What You Can't: Learning to Accept What You Are: The Complete Guide to Successful Self-improvement,* Nicholas Brealey Publishing, 2007

Shamon, Stella, *Real Wealth Creation*, Orion, 1999

Tolle, Eckhart, *The Power of Now*, Hodder & Stoughton, 2001

Williams, Nick, *Powerful Beyond Measure,* Bantam, 2004

Williams, Nick, *The Work We Were Born To Do*, Element, 2000

Williamson, Marianne, *A Return to Love*, Harper Collins, 1996

Woodhall, Ann Marie, *Secrets of a High-Heeled Healer*, HarperCollins, 2003

Woodroffe, Simon, *Book of Yo!*, Capstone, 2000

Acknowledgements

I wouldn't be writing this book if it weren't for Rachel Pryor, one of the most skilled and brilliant coaches in the world. She was my very first coach, and it was Rachel who introduced me to the concepts of scams and beliefs and has helped me formulate many of the ideas for this book. She has changed my life.

A huge thanks to all my wonderful Big Leapers: Nicky, Lynne, Rachel, Andrew, Marc, Tracy, Anne, Keris, Ann, Jules and Irene. Your courage and magnificence has inspired me on every page. You have been a joy to coach. Thank you to all the unidentified Big Leapers, too – I know who you are, and I take my hat off to you.

I would also like to thank all my coaches throughout my journey: Doug Scroggins, Harriet Simon Salinger, Nick Williams, Arlene Mann and Gabriella Goddard. Your inspiration and wisdom have helped me transform my life.

Big thanks to Ginny Baillie and Talene Miedaner for their help with my last-minute panic when writing about needs. For more information on Talene's work visit: www.lifecoach.com.

This book would never have been written without the wisdom of the founder of Coach University, Thomas Leonard.

Thanks to Fiona Spencer Thomas for all her help getting this project started.

Thanks to Aruna Vasudevan and the team at New Holland Publishers for their enthusiasm and belief in me.

Thanks to Martha Beck for her inspiration on the journalistic exercises. Read her book *Finding Your Own North Star: Claiming the Life You Were Meant to Live* for more inspiration on making your Big Leap.

I wouldn't be sane if it weren't for my good friends Nicky, Rachel, Nick M, Ros and Steve, Claire Power (and the lovely Barry), Carolyn, Caroline and to the lovely Claire R for being a total star, and making me laugh when all I wanted to do was cry.

And a big kiss to my own Inner Coach, who finally managed to speak up enough for this process to be as enjoyable as writing a book could be.

Index